NURTURING
silence IN A
NOISY *heart*

NURTURING
silence IN A
NOISY *heart*

how to find inner peace

wayne e. oates

Augsburg
MINNEAPOLIS

NURTURING SILENCE IN A NOISY HEART
How To Find Inner Peace

First published 1979 by Doubleday & Company, Inc.

Scripture quotations unless otherwise noted are from the New Revised Standard Version Bible, copyright © 1989 by the Division of Christian Education of the National Council of the Churches of Christ in the U.S.A. and used by permission.

Scripture quotations noted NEB are from *The New English Bible*, copyright © 1961, 1970 by the Delegates of the Oxford University Press and the Syndics of the Cambridge University Press. Reprinted by permission.

Cover and interior design by David Meyer

ISBN 0-8066-2037-4

The paper used in this publication meets the minimum requirements of American National Standard for Information Sciences—Permanence of Paper for Printed Library Materials, ANSI Z329.48-1984.   ∞

Manufactured in the U.S.A.   AF 9-2037

00	99	98	97	96	1	2	3	4	5	6	7	8	9	10

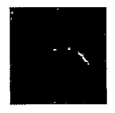

CONTENTS

PREFACE

Our hearts are noisy arenas. We have fightings within and fears without. Our inner conflicts make enough noise to keep us awake struggling over the dilemmas of decision-making. These noises drain our strength and sense of direction. Therefore, the idea that we can nurture silence in these noisy hearts of ours comes as good news. The disciplines of this nurturing are what this book is all about. Nurturing silence is something you can do for yourself; you can enjoy it. You can be strengthened from within by the confidence a silence spirit can give you. The wisdom of God comes to you and me, not in earthquake, wind, and fire, but in a still, small voice.

In addition to the noise of our inner conflicts are the literal noises of our external environment. Surface traffic, airplanes, ambulances, fire trucks, construction and demolition work, the chatter of crowds, the sounds of television, radios, and computers, and much more generate noise within our hearts. One purpose of this book is to encourage you to seek out solitude, quietness, and silence. Especially, my hope is that you and I will learn the discipline of pausing and listening to the silences that occur in the midst of a noisy world. For example, I was rushing to get to a class one day when I stopped at the kitchen sink to get a glass of orange juice. Out the window I saw a female cardinal sitting on a tree limb. At just that moment a male cardinal landed by her. He had a worm in his mouth. He placed it in her mouth and lovingly rubbed each side of her bill with his bill. Then he flew away. In less than a minute he returned with another worm for her, accompanied by his loving strokes. This ritual occurred about five times. I stood transfixed in total silence with my attention screening out everything else except this one drama before me. What a gift!

This book will help you sense what a powerful impact silence has on your whole being and outlook on life—both in your inner being and your interaction with the world around you. I also hope it will help you become a more meditative person. I cannot make meditation a full-time career; I must find it in the everyday world of action. Therefore, in this book I discuss the noises of the active life and the conflicts that consume us. We can become meditative, contemplative persons without escaping from this world; we can be down-to-earth while nurturing silence in a noisy heart.

chapter one

SILENCE

FOR SURVIVAL

AND HOPE

Camellias are not native to my part of the country; though they are one of the most delicate and beautiful flowers I know. Early one spring, long before the courageous jonquils bloom between ice and snow storms, a friend of ours sent us a box of many-colored camellias. She can grow camellias in our part of the country. She loves to do so. She takes the time, prepares a small greenhouse, and then makes room in her greenhouse for camellias to grow on their terms and not hers. She has a lot of respect for their terms of growth.

Silence is like camellias to me. Silence is not native to my world. Silence, more than likely, is a stranger to your world, too. If you and I are ever to have silence in our noisy hearts, we will have to grow it. Thus, when we nurture silence in our noisy hearts, we will do so on silence's terms for growth— terms that are not yet our own. You can nurture silence in your noisy heart if you value it, cherish it, and are eager to nourish it as my friend does her camellias.

For example, writing this book has often been an experiment in silence amid the mainstream of my noisy world. As I write this page, I am in my most silent place—at my desk at home—at the quietest time—it is five a.m. I am the farthest from noise I will be during the day. I can hear the pulse beat in my left ear. That is louder than the noise of distant traffic driving down the freeway. As a result, starting to write these words presents me with an obstacle course similar to the one facing you us you start nurturing silence in your noisy heart.

In my usual fashion I put that first forbidding blank page into the typewriter, and then become aware of its noise. That noise would become a part of any thought, feeling, or intention my heart would produce. So I thought of using my dictaphone. What a laugh! Here I am writing a book on nurturing silence in a noisy heart, all the while listening to the noise of my own voice That is a caricature of the world you and I help make. Finally, I pick up a pen and begin to write. Except for a muffled sound of pressure on the paper, noise is at a minimum, and silence at a maximum.

I thank my wife, who has made this place where I work quiet. Silence is a camellia to her. She has a soft, quiet voice. She communicates more without words than with them. We both like it that way—most of the time. She guards my silence. I reverence hers. She had the telephones fixed so that they can be turned off or unplugged. What a gift of knowing the power of silence she possesses! What patience to listen to floods of words from me, only to respond with a brief, wise, well-worded sentence or two, such as, "You need to turn the engines of your mind off. Just rest and be quiet for a while."

Silence can be nurtured in the noisy heart. I know. I have a noisy heart. If I survive as a whole person, I must start this experiment in nurturing silence. Join me.

Maybe your life and work—in their own special way—are similar to mine. When I worked in a walk-in clinic, I lived in noise all day. The sounds and events of those days are still very present in my mind. Police wrestle to handcuff a prisoner from the jail. He has just hit three people with his free hands. Screaming, banging, swearing, and crying fill the air. This happens outside my office door. The telephones ring incessantly. I respond to jangling telephone calls in a scramble of noise. A patient in pain and anger weeps and protests. The emergency medical team drives an ambulance to the emergency entrance of the hospital just outside our windows. Sirens shriek.

Police yell. Families at odds with each other raise their voices, hoping to get each other's attention. All the while, students need debriefing about events in their care of patients. Fellow staff members and I grab three minutes to talk with each other. We will be interrupted. Such events create a noisy uproar in hearts that pant for silence.

Yet, silence can be nurtured in the middle of all this noise. A co-worker not seen for a long time taps me on the shoulder, shakes my hand, gently presses my elbow, moves on and says nothing. A secretary quietly closes my office door to shut out noise and interruption. A patient says, "Before we start talking, can we just be quiet for a while? I need to catch my breath." A doctor weeps with me as we have just heard of the suicide of someone for whom we have been caring. In the large, noisy eating places a nurse, a doctor, or an aide fills her tray, sits down tired, and quietly bows her head over the meal. Stealing a glance, I sense the Presence of the One who hears. That One is heard by shutting out the noise that enters the heart, so that silence can be and is nurtured in the noisy heart—no matter where you and I are.

In order to get our bearings in the discovery of the seeds for nurturing silence and its conditions of growth in our noisy hearts, let's see if what I mean by "silence," and "a noisy heart" are close to what you mean.

The Messages of Silence

Silence is the absence of noise or speech. Silence is also something you can do. You can silence your tongue. You can just hush! More harshly said, you can shut up! I recall our first-born son, when he was three years old. He had a habit of telling everyone to shut up on any or all occasions. Finally, after friendly persuasion, firm commands, and placing my hand over his mouth, I told him in my despair, "Son! You're going to have to shut up saying 'Shut up!'" With a sense of seeming relief at the limits set, he mysteriously silenced himself of the habit. One day, several weeks later, I heard him whispering to himself and laughing gleefully. I asked him what was funny. He said, "I have found out that I can say 'Shut up' to myself and nobody minds!"

Silence is something you can do for yourself and even enjoy. The noisy heart can do things to you; you can nurture silence in your heart. You can do something about it.

Silence is something you hunt for. You rarely find it in a pure state. For example, where would you find the most silence in your everyday life? Simply being alone in total solitude during a day, a week, a month, or a year is a luxury. Yet, in order to grow silence in a noisy heart, such solitude—like my friend's greenhouse—is necessary to our very being, our survival. We can't wait for a cloistered cathedral, a dearly-paid-for room by the seaside, a yearned for walk in an ancient forest, an untouched wilderness. We need silence now. Drs. Meyer Friedman and Ray Rosenman say, ". . . to achieve things worth being usually requires long periods of solitude. . . . To be alone requires a place where you can be alone." They tell the story of a Texas friend who has a plush office and lives in a mansion. Yet "in order to find solitude . . . he regularly visits a mausoleum that he had built for himself and his wife."[1] That is as near as one can get to digging one's own grave for a short space of silence—though silence as deep as death is not exactly what most of us are looking for, is it?

On the contrary, we feel like Pascal, who said, "The eternal silence of the infinite spaces terrifies me."[2] We run from silence because we meet our real selves there. To do so scares us. We have too much terror as it is to look for silence in the graveyard of our inner selves.

I look for silence in several places. First, I look for silence in my own mind when I fix my attention on one object, one person, or one thought at a time. The world around us is a constant bombardment of multiple demands for your and my attention. The decision to listen to one person at a time, to focus attention on one object at a time, to concentrate on one thought at a time goes a long way toward silencing the many other contenders for attention.

Another way of finding a place of silence is to peel away all that is artificial or invented in the world of sound to observe and listen to that which basic nature presents us. John Keats describes:

> I stood tiptoe upon a little hill,
> The air was cooling and so very still
> . . . and then there crept
> A little noiseless noise among the leaves
> Born of the very sigh that silence heaves. . . .
> Linger a while upon some bending planks
> That lean against a streamlet's rushy banks,
> And watch intently Nature's gentle doings:
> They will be found softer than ring-doves' cooings
> How silent comes the water round that bend,
> Not the minutest whisper does it send. . . .[3]

Such an event puts all artificial noises out of the range of awareness and enables silence to grow in the noisy heart.

Yet, the world of the natural is alive with sound—the rustle of the wind, the music of birds, the cries of animals, the creaking of tree limbs, and the crash of ocean waves. These sounds are different from and more desirable than the screech of tires, the honking of horns, the rumble of trucks, and the roar of jet engines. They make us feel like the poet Lord Byron, when he wrote:

> There is a pleasure in the pathless woods,
> There is rapture on the lonely shore,
> There is society where none intrudes,
> By the deep Sea, and music in its roar;
> I love not man less, but Nature more.[4]

Such pleasure stands in contrast with what my friend Bill Oshenski gives as a description of hell: His idea of hell is to be caught in a traffic jam driving a subcompact car. In front of him is a large bus belching diesel fumes into his air vents. On the sides of him are two semitrailer trucks racing their engines in stereo! And all creating the kind of hell in unwanted silence which Rachel Carson details in her book *Silent Spring*.[5] She describes the devastation of nature for humanity's own ends. The result is the silenced voices of spring in countless American communities. This silence is too absolute to be natural. It is the silence of an old battlefield, like the stillness at Appomattox, Gettysburg, Normandy Beach. Perfect silence is rarely found. Once I chanced to converse with a trio of folk singers. They were highly educated, expressive, attractive persons—two young men and a lovely young lady. We were discussing music, sound, and silence, and they told me of an experiment with silence which they had conducted. They had a group sit in as nearly perfect silence as humanly possible in a relatively soundproof music room. After a long time of listening to the silence, they began to report what they had sensed. Almost unanimously they reported hearing the building itself move ever so slightly. They had heard the building popping, cracking—almost moving restlessly! Their experience echoes the mood of Thomas Merton:

> Be still
> Listen to the stones of the wall.
> Be silent, they try
> To speak your
>
> Name.
> Listen
> To the living walls.
> Who are you?
> Who
>
> Are you? Whose
> Silence are you?
>
> Who (be quiet)
> Are you (as these stones
> Are quiet.) . . .[6]

Silence speaks out of the "unalive" world of walls, then. Merton belonged to the Trappist order of Catholic monks in the Abbey of

Gethsemani. Silence is a part of the rule of obedience which they follow. This does not mean, however, that the "monk must *never* go out, *never* receive a letter, *never* have a visitor, *never* talk to anyone, *never* hear any news. He must distinguish what is useless and harmful from what is useful and salutary, and *in all things* glorify God."[7] (Author's italics.)

He uses the word "distinguish." What does that mean about silence? Wrapped up in "distinguish" is the basic principle of nurturing silence in a noisy heart. It means to "choose between" or to "choose from among" the many sounds—noises, tones, words—what is useful in creating within us a clean heart and a right spirit. We put to the test all that we are about to say or not say; we are constantly choosing to listen, and choosing what we will listen to. We develop, under the tutelage of the Spirit of God, the power to discern and make choices in the feeding, nurturing, and growing of our personal realm of silence. Jesus suggests a kind of prayer that is not known for its "much speaking." He taught simplicity of utterance. Your "yes" is to be "yes" and your "no" is to be "no." Silence, then, is not just not talking. Silence is a discipline of choosing what to say and to what to listen. Nurturing silence, then, is the growth of the power of discernment as to what will be the focus of your attention, care, and commitment.

If you limit what you say to what is true, if you limit yourself to what can be spoken in love, then you will have much less to say. What you do say, though, will have a hundred times more influence. If you limit, change, or expand the objects of your attention (your listening), you can become the kind of person you want to be, change the kinds of directions in which you want to go.

Rarely do you and I experience total silence. We decide what we are going to listen to at a given time. Thus we kill off other noises. Perfect silence is the exclusive realm of those who cannot hear and see. But the power of choice is taken from the deaf-blind. They have the luxury of not having to listen to the banal noises, superficial conversations, and cruel things people say. Yet the removal of the power to choose for oneself is a cruel fate for them. Helen Keller was deaf and blind from an incurable childhood disease. Anne Sullivan taught her to read through her senses of touch, smell, and taste. At the end of her autobiography Helen Keller says:

> Fate—silent, pitiless—bars the way. Fain would I question his imperious decree; for my heart is undisciplined and passionate, but my tongue will not utter the bitter, futile words that rise to my lips, and they fall back into my heart like unshed tears. Silence sits immense upon my soul. Then comes hope with a smile and whispers, "There is joy in self-forgetfulness." So I try to make the light in other people's eyes my sun, the musts in others' ears my symphony, the smile on others' lips my happiness.[8]

But you and I, before old age or the massive sensory overload deafens us, have a choice. The impact of a noisy world, the shouting of contrary voices within your heart, the loss of hearing due to age—all these press upon you the power to choose your own particular silence that—like camellias—you can make room for and enable to grow in your heart. Which raises the second question: What is a "noisy heart"?

The Noisy Heart

A noise is any sound that you do not want or that comes between you and something to which you have chosen to listen. Your wants are at the "heart" of you. The things you do not want to hear make a noisy heart for you. The things you listen to capture your attention. The things you listen to are those to which your deepest desires have committed your attention. Are they really worthwhile? The noises that keep you from listening, paying attention to, or even hearing what your heart desires can be screened out. What, then, will you listen to? Or, can you stand the silence?

"The noisy heart" has at least three meanings here. First, noise is the load of sound—chosen or unchosen—on your eardrums. Technical studies on noise give plenty of examples: the effects of machine-gun fire, artillery fire, and explosions of bombs on the ears of combat soldiers, leaving them with impaired hearing; the effects of traffic noises, trucks, cars, trains, sirens, and blowing horns—on the whole person as well as on one's hearing; the effects of jet-plane takeoffs, landings, and sonic booms—which have brought on heated arguments over the location of airports, the pathways of flights in the skyways, and whether bigger and noisier jets are to be permitted. Rock music, with its electronic multiplication of the volume of sound, especially in closed spaces, actually impairs the hearing of the listeners. Such examples constitute what we usually mean by the "load," the volume or intensity of sound.

A second meaning of noise "in the heart" is the annoyance levels of given noises. For example, the context of a given noise is a good index to its nuisance strength. A train, approaching with horn sounding, engines throbbing, and wheels clanking, sounds like music to your ears if you are awaiting the arrival of a beloved member of your family. The same train is an annoyance if it passes your home at three a.m. every Wednesday—often enough to awaken you, not often enough for you to become accustomed enough to the noise. The frame of meaning, value, satisfaction, and joy with which you surround a given noise rules it "in" as permissible or "out" as an annoyance.

Noise "in the heart," in the third place, means the friction that other people cause you in your daily life. I would call this between-folks noise. It may be caused by a physically silent event such as a person not speaking to you, giving you the cold shoulder, or simply giving you a disgusted dirty look.

Between-folks noise is the kind that goes straight to the heart with or without the human ear. It may arise from competitive, status-seeking and status-holding impasses. It may arise from long-standing differences in patterns and values in human situations. It may arise from situations in which enough vindictive distrust has grown up that any silencing of the turmoil is futile. Noise, particularly of the between-folks variety, changes heart and blood functions enough to start destroying rather than building your body and life. As one man said, "I have too much respect for my blood vessels to live in a place where I am constantly angry and angered." Nurturing silence in a noisy heart calls for digging around at the roots of what is going on between people.

Close examination of what is going on between you and other people will reveal the source of much noise in your heart. And such a noisy heart may be damaging the soil in which you have intended silence to grow. Therefore, some of your between-folks actions can be phrased into questions that will serve as a soil test for the nurturing of silence in your noisy heart.

1. *Have other persons made demands of you that are impossible, unfair, persistent and uninterrupted, or that you—left to the meditations of your own heart—would consider immoral, unethical?* If so, you have an anger, a confusion, a clotting conscience, and/or a struggle of indecision that destroys the serenity and quietness of your whole being. Letting the real you stand up and put an end to the racket by expressing your decision to say no to the demands of others is an experiment in the growth of silence and peace in a conflict-ridden heart. You may be lonely; you have silence; can you stand it? Or are you addicted to the other person's demands?

2. *Do other people give you contradictory messages?* For example, does someone call on you for help and say so in so many words—but then offer to pay you, and you get the feeling "in your heart" that the person sees her- or himself as helping you, thinking you can't make your own way? What a noise in your own heart! You feel uneasy, at a loss for words, and confusion boils within you. The double message must be silenced. Why not just say, "I will be glad to help you, if that is what I am doing. When you offer to pay me, though, are you trying to tell me that you are really wanting to help me? Do you think I can't make it without your help?" That would get the double message up on the table. It could be dealt with straightforwardly. The confusion would clear. The between-folks noise would be silenced.

3. *Do you have people in your life who are grown, healthy, and able to think but who nevertheless demand your full, around-the-clock attention?* If you are the mother of a newborn baby, you have the nearest equivalent to what I mean by around-the-clock attention. However, for a person who is eighteen, nineteen, thirty-four, or forty-six to demand your every waking thought is a "noise in the

heart." An extremely old relative or one who is disabled at any age presents the possibility of such demands. However, only God can give full-time attention to an individual. You are not God. Some distribution of attention—even with a newborn baby—has to be worked out. The nurse, the companion, the other relatives, the neighbors, the occasional visitor, are at work sharing such loads. But then, again, is your heart noisy because you cannot share the load?

Ordinarily, the person who demands your undivided attention is a son, a daughter, a parent, a friend, a wife or husband who is possessive, jealous, and without purpose other than you. You are filled with rage and disquietness. You both love and resent the person. You are a victim of your own good intentions. Putting the person out of your heart and mind is next to impossible for you. Yet for the person to take up all the room in your heart is equally impossible. You will need the wise help of a good friend, a counselor—such as a pastor, a teacher, a physician, a social caseworker—to extricate your noisy heart from this double bind. More than this—you will need resolve to stop the person from putting you in God's place in his or her life. You cannot permit anyone to demand attention that only God can give and that consumes you. Such a game is a deadly one in which people wind up in hospitals, divorce courts, and mortuaries.

God intends life, not death, for you and for the person whose demands fill you with discord in a noisy heart:

> For God alone my soul waits in silence;
>> from him comes my salvation.
> He only is my rock and my salvation,
>> my fortress; I shall never by shaken. [Psalm 62:1-2]

4. Are there past memories of painful betrayals, failures, or broken relationships that fill your heart with perpetual noise? Your life is a constant instant replay of old events that would have turned out differently if . . ., if . . . , if . . . You may have trouble forgiving others for their wrongdoing. You have more trouble forgiving yourself for being taken as a fool. You cannot quiet your noisy heart. In exhaustion, helplessness, and frustration you finally would call on God for some quieting of your spirit. Yet, when you think of doing so, you may have trouble even forgiving God for letting the whole mess happen in the first place.

Then will you go one step further? Realize that you are serving as judge, juror, jailer, and executioner. In a harsh and unforgiving way you are putting yourself in God's place. Are you the one who forgives God? Can you top that? If that is not ridiculous enough to make you laugh, then your sense of humor needs a new engine job! Laughter is, at times, a kind of forgiveness. Really, now! You have shut your heart and thrown the key away. You may not even like your own thoughts, as was the case with the psalmist:

> I am weary with my moaning;
>> every night I flood my bed with tears;
> I drench my couch with my weeping.
> My eyes waste away because of grief;
>> they grow weak because of all my foes. [Psalm 6:6-7]

The noise that comes from your heart comes in air filled with musty, mildewed odors. The sounds from your heart will be better when they are mediated through fresh air waves. Open up your heart to fresh breezes of new wisdom. Converse with someone who has a different angle of vision. You have gotten stuck with one angle of vision. Possibly another person's perspective will be a breath of fresh air for your noisy heart, allowing you to have a "change of heart" from noise to the serenity that silence can bring—the silencing of demands, double messages, possessive people in your life, and the painful memories you replay.

You are right. Such changes call for a specific understanding of your heart. People say, "If I know my own heart . . ." Have you taken a close look at your heart and asked several questions?

1.   *Is my heart open and teachable?* Jesus used the word "heart" to mean what you and I mean when we say "head." In Matthew 19:8 Jesus speaks of "your hardness of heart"; the New English Bible translates this, "your minds were closed," and the Jerusalem Bible, "you were so unteachable." This closedness and unteachableness can

well be called hard-headedness. It is the opposite of what Paul spoke of when he said, "Be generous to one another, tender-hearted, forgiving one another as God in Christ forgave you" (Ephesians 4:32 NEB). However you translate it, the meaning is the same: Can you learn anything from other people; do you have the capacity to put yourself in other people's places and understand how they feel?

2. *Is my heart cast down? Have I lost courage?* The word "courage" comes from the Latin word for "heart." To lose heart means to become discouraged, disheartened. To overcome fear and regain your courage means to be encouraged. Jesus referred to this frequently, as when he said, "Set your troubled hearts at rest. Trust in God always; trust also in me" (John 14:1, NEB).

3. *Examine closely what you mean when you use the word "heart."* Take a sheet of paper and write down what you mean by "heart." Do you mean courage? With heart, you are encouraged. When you "lose heart," you are discouraged. Do you mean kindness and say, "Have a heart"? Thus you urge another person to be kind or generous. Do you mean a sense of challenge, initiative, and purpose? When all of that goes out of your job, your marriage, etc., do you say, "I can do this, but my heart is not in it?" Do you mean your capacity to remember, as when you learn some things "by heart"? Is this what you mean? Or, do you mean the feeling of rejection, shame, and total put-down you have received at the mercilessness of another person? You may say, "I was doing fine until he or she cut the heart out of me." Others would say, "I was cut to the 'quick'!"

Many times when you use the word "heart," you mean the central issue, the bottom line, the crux of a matter. You have "gotten to the heart" or center of things. Purity of heart enables you and me to see God. Søren Kierkegaard, a Danish poet-philosopher of the nineteenth century, spoke of purity of heart as "willing one thing," of having a singular purpose in the love of God and neighbor. He insisted that your and my human cleverness be used to cut out all evasions of commitment, to prevent both the external and internal deceptions that contaminate the heart with the noise of competing loyalties, commitments, and devotions. Commitment is a whole hearted decision, and a person cannot "by the craft and the flattery of tongue lay hold of God while his heart is far away." Or, in another place in the same work, "As the sea, when it lies calm and deeply transparent, yearns for heaven, so may the pure heart when it is calm and deeply transparent yearn for the Good."[9]

You are likely to say, "Am I to pull myself together in what Kierkegaard calls 'purity of heart' all alone?" You may ask of God the same question the psalmist did:

> Why, O Lord, do you stand far off?
> Why do you hide yourself in times of trouble? [Psalm 10:1]

You may resent the silence of God, "whose voice is not heard." You may want an audible voice in response to your prayer. As difficult as it is to get hold of, "deep speaks unto deep" in your relationship to God. As you quiet your shrill-pitched demands, you experience the deeper reaches of your own heart. You come to know God in that stillness. As you cease the need to scream, shout, and demand, the very peace and quiet you experience blends into the stillness of God's Presence.

Then watch out! You will think thoughts that you have not thought before. The silence you cultivate becomes the medium of fresh wisdom from the Creator.

chapter two

DISCOVERING

YOUR PRIVACY IN ORDER

TO NURTURE SILENCE

A street that ends at a riverbank may well be a dead end. Some of them are. Such a street could be eroded away inch by inch by different flood stages of the river. Another possibility is that the end of the street may be bounded by a riverfront drive on which you can turn right or left, making the street part of the regular public thoroughfare. Another possibility is that the street could run smoothly off into the water and become a slip for launching boats, especially houseboats. Thus it could be an avenue to the expanses of the river.

Think of living on such a street. On the street there are many people. Either cars whiz by, or the street is so poorly paved that cars avoid it. If the street is a dead end, only other people living on the street and those visiting them travel it. In any of these cases, the amount of privacy you have is different. Furthermore, the only way you could have total privacy would be to own or rent the whole street. I suppose that would be out of the question. However, you could own a houseboat. If your street slipped off as a launching ramp into a river, you could go down the street, get on your houseboat, and then go to the quietest part of the river. You would have privacy on your terms as the result of your investment in a houseboat. You adventured and invested to discover a place of privacy where cars do not go by, where telephones cannot reach you, and where you will not feel observed at all times.

In brief, to discover privacy for the nurturing of silence today calls for investment and a sense of adventure.

If you can, with ingenuity, inventiveness, and courage, discover your own working model for privacy. Then having found privacy itself, let us—you and me—collaborate in the rest of this chapter. Go with me. Devise avenues to privacy for the nurturing of silence in your noisy heart and mine.

Privacy: A Discovery after Adventure

If you are to nurture silence, privacy is a treasure that must be found. To find privacy in a crowded world such as yours is an adventure in its own right. Yet you may be one of those people who shuns privacy. If so, why not examine some of your own behaviors and learn to identify the need for privacy, because the need for privacy must be felt before you seek it. In order to feel the need, you can use some premonitory signs of the approaching urge for privacy.

Preludes to Privacy

Fatigue. The most obvious kind of privacy you experience is sleep. Fatigue is a prelude to sleep. Fatigue in the ordinary course of human life, then, is a good warning sign. Fatigue lets you know that you need some privacy.

Fatigue, however, is more than just being tired. It means that the cells of your body have become so depleted that you have lost vitality and the capacity to respond. Fatigue is to be wearied from extended and excessive effort. Jesus had such an experience. He and his disciples came to a village in Samaria and sat down at a well that Jacob had given to his son Joseph. The Scripture says that Jesus was wearied. Upon becoming this wearied, Jesus sat alone at the well. His disciples apparently were getting something for all of them to eat. When they returned, they urged him to eat. For a brief time, nonetheless, Jesus was alone. He sat at the well during the least likely time of day for people to come to the well—high noon. When he was fatigued, he sought privacy. Therefore you can feel kinship with Jesus when you use fatigue as a warning signal to seek privacy.

Where and when do you get the most completely fatigued in your day, week month, year? Write down your schedule and plan for some open spaces for privacy at those times. That way you anticipate your need for privacy and make provisions for it.

Loss of Perspective. Another warning signal alerting you to search for privacy is the loss of perspective. Perspective means that you have the capacity to see or view persons and things in their true relationship to each other. You see things as they are, not in some distorted manner. The person who has lost his or her perspective is one who gets to the point where he or she cannot see the woods for the trees. Fatigue contributes to this. A deep disappointment in or fear of another person will become the center of your vision. Instead of seeing things in your accustomed perspective, you will see them darker or brighter than they really are. You are either down in the dumps or reassuring yourself too much. The most telltale evidence of the loss of perspective is when you begin to belabor the point in discussion, "sweat the small stuff" in decision-making, procrastinate about big decisions, or become inappropriately irritable with your fellow workers, your family, or your friends. You are making too many mistakes. You need privacy.

Poor Judgment. A very dangerous warning signal for you to begin to seek some privacy is when you begin to exercise poor judgment. Good judgment means you are able to draw reliable conclusions from materials you have acquired by experience in the past, to profit by past mistakes. This is critical judgment. It means that you can tell the difference between right and wrong and act accordingly, choose the paths of action that are in the best interest of yourself and of those for whom you are responsible. Critical judgment also means that you make decisions that are in tune with your long-term obligations and not simply tuned to the impulses of the moment. Your critical judgment is becoming impaired when you make impulse decisions detrimental to your own and other special persons' best interest.

Another kind of judgment is what we call reflex judgment. For example, if a wet towel is swung at your face, then your eyes, your whole head, and neck muscles jump away in reflex movement. This kind of judgment is very important if you are operating machinery, or making reflex judgments concerning your own and other persons' health and welfare. The person who is going through a severe marital conflict may, therefore, be well advised to be very careful in operating a car. The stress of such a situation is connected with some automobile accidents. Less dramatically, you can notice your impairment of reflex judgment in the increase of the number of small mistakes you make in a day. You are likely to catch yourself: "This is just one of those days I should not have gotten out of bed!" Your whole being is calling for a cessation of activity, for the kind of rest and renewal that comes to you if you provide space for some privacy for yourself. Lower the number of responsibilities you have in the day. Drop out of sight of some of the people you see daily. Poor judgment, either of your critical capacities or your reflex judgment, is a two-, three-, or four-alarm indication that you need some time to yourself, some privacy.

Confusion of Heart. Confusion of heart occurs when you are trapped in the double bind of a double mind. You feel equally drawn to each of two or more options for living. You become unstable in your path of action because of the double bind: You want to do all these things but must choose one. Consequently, while you wait and ponder, stall for time, live in a fantasy, and procrastinate, you find your life falling into disorder around you. The noisy heart has engulfed your surroundings. Disorder reigns. Someone says, "You fiddle while Rome burns." You agree. You can feel that the heat is on. Your life is in shambles. You are unstable in all your ways. You are now not simply feeling the need for privacy—the whole life situation thrown around you is demanding it. Search for some privacy now!

The Stuff of which Privacy Is Made

Of what does privacy for you consist? What is the stuff of which privacy is made?

Loneliness

When you silence the clatter of the fatigue, loss of perspective, poor judgment, and confusion of heart with privacy, you are facing the first ingredient of privacy: loneliness. Thomas Wolfe said, "Loneliness, far from being a rare and curious phenomenon, peculiar to myself and a few other solitary men is the central, inevitable fact of human existence."[1] Serious psychologists have insisted that you and I are met with two overwhelming feelings when we consider our place in the world of human action: loneliness and ecstasy. I feel that the loneliness precedes the ecstasy. If you are afraid of the loneliness and shrink back from the adventure of searching for privacy because of it, you will drop back into the drabness of the four great noises of the human heart—fatigue, loss of perspective, poor judgment, and confusion—which are the preludes to privacy. The failure of nerve is to lose your spirit of life, your taste for life, and to remain overloaded with these low aimed muddly feelings. Face loneliness unafraid.

Freedom from the Crowd

Jesus sought freedom from the crowd. He left the crowd that was clamoring for a continuation of the miracles of bread. They could not find him. After his inaugural message at Nazareth, the crowd became so angry that they rose up to put him out of the city. But he passed through the middle of the crowd and "went away." He had compassion on the crowd, because they were harassed and helpless, like sheep without a shepherd. However, he could say, "This is a lonely place, and the hour is now late; send the crowds away so that they may go into the villages . . ." (Matthew 14:13-15). Extensive references point to his necessity to be free from the crowd. The necessity lies in the fickleness of the crowd mind. The same crowd that cheered Jesus on his triumphal entry into Jerusalem was apparently present when he was crucified and, in fact, in some instances cried, "Crucify him!" Gustave LeBon says that one of the most striking peculiarities of a psychological crowd is:

> Whoever be the individuals that compose it, however like or unlike be their mode of life, their occupations, their character, or their intelligence, the fact that they have been transformed into a crowd puts them in possession of a sort of collective mind which makes them feel, think and act in a manner quite different from that in which each individual of them would feel, think, and act were he in a state of isolation.[2]

If Jesus were ever to become that individual whom he knew himself to be, and thereby actually to exercise the wisdom that came to him from God, then he would have to free himself from the crowd. He was not an other-directed person, moving with the tides of the crowd's reactions. He was free of the crowd.

An element of the stuff from which privacy is made is freedom from the crowd. Your very emotional and spiritual health relies upon that freedom. Depression scores rank significantly higher for persons living in crowded rather than uncrowded areas. High residential crowding is more common in lower-middle and middle income groups than in extreme poverty groups. "Crowding is . . . a major factor associated with increased symptomatology." So says a careful study made by Dr. John Schwab and others.[3]

The Right to Private Thought and Judgment

You not only have a responsibility to have a private thinking process and a set of private judgments that amount to convictions for you yourself—you also have a right to be allowed such privacy. That right is an essential element in your search for privacy. Go after it!

As early as Edward Coke (1552-1624), English writers on the common law said that no person, ecclesiastical or temporal, shall be examined upon secret thoughts of his heart or of his secret opinion. However, many persons today have no sense of their own personal space, their own inner privacy. They have trouble, for example, knowing the difference between their parents' opinions and their own. They have difficulty deciding what their own opinions are and what those of their public are. Parents and public officials insist on their own privacy rights but consider it nothing at all to invade the private thoughts of their sons and daughters or their constituency. As a result, the decrease of individuality and the loss of a clear-cut sense of personal selfhood breaks open into a general fear and distrust of parents and public officials

Sir Thomas More (1478-1535) was pushed and shoved by his friends, by Henry VIII, and finally by his own family to divulge his own opinion of Henry's divorce and remarriage. Yet, says Robert Bolt of him:

> He knew where he began and left off, what area of himself he could yield to the encroachments of his enemies, and what to the encroachments of those he loved . . . at length he was asked to retreat from that final area where he located his self. And there this supple, humorous, unassuming, and sophisticated person set like metal, was overtaken by an absolute primitive rigor, and could no more be budged than a cliff.[4]

More insisted on the right to have his own private opinion of King Henry's divorce, to keep his silence. He resigned from his office. In Bolt's play about him, though, Cromwell says of More, "That silence of his is bellowing up and down Europe!" More says to his own wife, ". . . in silence is my safety under the law, but my silence must be absolute, it must extend to you."[5] She felt that he did not trust her. He insisted that he was protecting her from having to testify against him if indeed she were ever asked and required to say that which he had said to her.

Yet this silence and inner privacy left him alone, absolutely alone before God.

Courage of Companionship with God Alone

The central component of privacy is the courage that arises from the inner persuasion that God is with you when all others leave. The awareness of the presence of God provides a sense of companionship and turns loneliness into solitude. Furthermore, it makes total privacy an adventure into ethical responsibility Your own convictions about what your responsibilities are guide you, not merely the preconventional survival and convenience levels of moral commitment, not the conventional levels of being a "good man"/"nice woman," not simply obeying external law and order. It goes even beyond the higher reaches of morality in social contracts or universal ethical principles. Companionship with God goes to the level of relationship with an ethical God who reveals to you a wisdom that informs and humbles you at the same time. What you think and its resulting actions become a matter of integrity for you as a personal self, a matter of serenity in your inner being against a noisy, conflict-ridden, conscience-stricken heart.

The Conditions Conducive to Privacy

Such inner reflection as I have described in naming the stuffs of which privacy is made becomes possible in your own private wilderness. When Moses fled for his life from Egypt, he fled to a wilderness. The privacy he experienced there was surrounded by the silence of the hills and the valleys, and was punctuated only by his work as a shepherd. Amos, the eighth-century prophet, was an inhabitant of the wilderness. Jesus marshaled his courage and spent forty days and forty nights in the wilderness, alone before God. He resolved the noises of conflicting demands about the way he would spend the next three years of his life. The apostle Paul, after his dramatic conversion experience and his conversation with Ananias at Damascus, went for the silent years of his life into the Arabian desert. Since then, and with these persons as an example, persons like St. Anthony in the desert, John Bunyan in prison, and Roger Williams in exile have had their own particular shift-out from the crowd around them. They found a place of rejection and a station in life that created the conditions of a private world for them.

A Place of Privacy: What Is the Wilderness for You?

You are confronted with the necessity of deciding what is your particular wilderness. What place or situation in life makes silence a reality? What place gives you freedom from the clamoring noise of other people's opinions, peering eyes, and demanded expectations? I have been asking this question of myself. I find that a certain chair in the living room of my home, even at times of day when interruptions of every kind are happening, provides a measure of quietness that I cannot find elsewhere. In fact, home itself is a place of quietness that I do not find elsewhere. Even when our grown sons were small children, this was true. I think this reflects the quality of selfhood that my wife possesses—whose way of life breathes serenity and silent peacefulness. The home she has created has been a constant nurturing of silence in the noisy hearts of her husband and sons.

In addition, the large city has for the length of my life been the wilderness into which I have retreated. I am persuaded that many people today find anonymity, the combined feverish search for a little peace and quiet from the crowd, and the opportunity to wander from one place to another unobserved in the heart of large cities themselves. The maze of the large city is for us often the modern equivalent of the wilderness for Moses, Amos, Jesus, and Paul. You do not have to find a Mojave Desert, a mountain resort, a rockbound seacoast fishing village, or a pathless woods to have a place of privacy and solitude.

Yet many persons do find their place of privacy close to unspoiled nature spots. You may be one of them. A surgeon who operates on many persons in open-heart surgery says that farmers tend to face that kind of surgery with more tranquillity and less noise of anxiety than do persons in other occupations. He attributes this to the way of life the person has been living—close to the elements of nature: He or she does not argue with the weather, assumes that the laws of nature are to be both depended upon and respected, and does not fret nearly as much as a result.

The critical question for you in creating the conditions of privacy for the purpose of nurturing silence is: What is your equivalent of the wilderness? You can decide that. Do not let someone else decide it for you. If it can be easily accessible, it is better. Jesus said that a person should go into his or her closet to pray. This is an "inner chamber," a private room. The trouble with letting your place of privacy be a distant wilderness is that you will always think of your place for nurturing silence as somewhere other than where you are. Hence the nurturing of silence will not be daily. Or you will think of nurturing silence as calling for a change of your whole routine into a totally new way of life. People have done the latter. I have known persons, such as a professor at the university where I worked, who have quietly reworked all their priorities over a span of time, left the rat race of academia or the business world and moved to a simplified, rural existence that became their "Walden" retreat. I know other persons, such as Clarence Jordan who in the late 1930s planned his whole life career with the building of a spiritual community of integrated black-and-white communal living in Americus, Georgia.

Yet neither the rural nor the urban alternative for a periodic place of solitude seems workable for many persons. For eleven summers I taught in New York City and left my home base to do so. The city itself provided a time of solitude, renewed perspective, and inner reflection for me. Yet, I must confess, the rigors of moving back and forth were as noise producing as could be. After we got settled in, it worked fine. However, the double transition in a short span of six or seven weeks was a special stress in its own right. I am more aware, therefore, of your need to build such a place of silence into your ordinary routine in life. The exploration of your timing and your scheduling of your life is what you probably need most to do.

The Time and Timing of Privacy

Jesus not only had a wilderness as a place he could go to settle the noisy heart that filled him, he also chose specific times. He escaped the crowd often. He arose while it was not yet day. We have no record of his remaining awake late, although he may well have done so. Yet we can derive the principle of time and timing as one way he took to nurture silence in his heart, to give himself to prayer, and to focus the great decisions of his life. You have some command over your schedule, so you can shift the schedule of your life to some degree.

I recall the story of Douglas Southall Freeman as told to me by a mutual friend. He said that this busy editor of the Richmond, Virginia, *Times Dispatch* regularly arose at four o'clock each morning. He would go straight to his office after having a light breakfast. He would read, meditate, study, and reflect upon his writing assignments. He would rearrange the emphases of his life. He would think through the commitments of the day. Then he would enter into his regular appointment schedule at nine a.m.. He usually would eat a light lunch in his office and then stay at his desk until two p.m. Then he would go home and redress for bed, go to bed, and sleep two to three hours. Subsequently he arose for the second time of the day, then read his stack of other newspapers while he awaited his dinner hour. He was then free to eat dinner with his wife and children and spend the forepart of the evening conversing with them. He went to bed around nine or ten p.m. Thus he had plenty of time for meditation, reflection, silence, and total quiet at times of day when everyone else was doing something else. In fact, he did everything, except that which he chose to do with others, at some other time than that which people ordinarily do it. As a result he was able to get two days out of one and plenty of rest at the same time.

Douglas Southall Freeman, however, was a professional man. You may be a shift worker. If you have the choice of shift, you can often find more solitude on an evening or a late-night and early-morning shift than on the day shift. When I worked in industry, I found that the night shift provided an opportunity for personal solitude that no other time did. When I was a night watchman in college, I found the serenity and quietness of other people's sleeping time to be a choice time for centering down my life in silence. When I worked in a medical school and its associated hospitals, I found that rotating into and out of different shifts got the work done and, at the same time, provided me with expanses of opportunity to be alone, to adventure into privacy, and to cultivate silence in my life.

Thomas Merton spoke of contemplation in a world of action. Your world is, more likely than not, one of action. You look for the green pastures and still waters of silence to heal your noisy heart in the middle of a hectic existence. Quelling chaos is probably the name of the game of your life. Consequently, the disciplined use of time to outwit the noise both without and within is a way to find the place of quietness in the place of noise at a time much of the noise is somewhere else.

I cannot tune time to your temperament for you. You should write down what your typical day's schedule tends to be like, and then begin landscaping the schedule to create some places and times of privacy for your regular cultivation of silence, communion with your inner being, and communion with the Eternal in your noisy heart.

Some Quiet Motions of the Spirit that Nurture Silence

Now that you have discovered privacy and been given the courage to face it by the knowledge of the presence of God, you say, "OK. Here I am. This is it. I have privacy. I feel lonely as all get out. I am resisting the first fifteen temptations to go find somebody to talk with or find some task to do to get my mind off this being alone business. What's this stuff about nurturing silence in my noisy heart all about? What is my heart supposed to be up to at this time and in this place of privacy?" Good question. Your inner self has some motions of the spirit that serve as disciplines or actions for the quieting of the noisy heart. You can use them yourself.

Standing Apart

Ecstasy is an entrancing joy. It means to "stand outside of" or "to stand apart from," if you use its most literal meaning. Let's use the most literal one. You have been engrossed in a demanding set of problems. You have lost perspective, you are fatigued, you have made some errors of judgment, you are confused. Now you have a time of privacy and a place for personal companionship with God. You deliberately choose to acknowledge your fatigue, poor perspective, errors of judgment, and confusion. You push yourself away and stand apart from the demanding set of problems. You center down on silence as a way of hushing the clatter of demands. You can do this by deliberately getting up and moving from where you are. Imagine that you have left the set of problems in the place from which you have moved. Therefore, you stand apart from them. You concentrate on the persons who are demanding and the problems that you have faced as if they were a movie. You are not in it. You are standing apart from it. Your "part" is being played by a good actor, a good actor who is not you. You make an appraisal of your thoughts and actions in the situation, in the drama, in the movie you are watching as if it were not you. I learned this discipline from a young American soldier who had fought in Vietnam, who said that in battle he watched the tracer bullets of his machine gun as if they were a multicolored movie, as if he were not there. Thus he could survive.

Your life may be a battle of contending forces. The rattle and noise of battle weighs your heart down. You stand apart from it. You reappraise it. You deliberately desensitize the pain and noise by watching the course of your life situation as a not-you. This turns the stranger in your heart to your advantage. After all, these pressures and problems, put into the perspective of eternity, will pass away, too. You may note the ludicrous, funny aspects of your own behavior. Instead of coughing with embarrassment, as you usually do when you catch a glimpse of yourself in action without intending to, you laugh at the funny dimensions of it all. You are not a character actor here; you are really the clown! That is not bad humor! All the while you were taking yourself as seriously as death, you were really clowning!

But you will say to me, "Knock it off! This is not funny. This is grim business, being alone: trying to put up with the silence, facing myself as I am, standing apart from myself. It scares me." Then I offer the guidance of Dag Hammarskjöld:

> When all becomes silent around you, and you recoil in terror—see that your work has become a flight from suffering and responsibility, your unselfishness a thinly disguised masochism; hear, throbbing within you the

spiteful, cruel heart of the steppe wolf—do not then anesthetize yourself by once again calling up the shouts and horns of the hunt, but gaze steadfastly at the vision until you have plumbed its depths.[6]

Backing Off

Another discipline that helps to nurture silence is backing off—reducing the amount of initiative you use in social situations, placing initiative in other people's hands, reducing some of your pushiness that confuses your relationships with other people, relaxing some of your demands upon other people, and standing back to let others do a few things for a while. Much fatigue, loss of perspective, poor judgment, and confusion of heart comes from being over involved in other people's lives. These persons may be adult members of your family. They may be co-workers on your job who have come to mean the wrong thing to you, to mean more to you than a co-worker can comfortably mean, and to preoccupy your waking day thoughts. In your time of privacy, reassess this as over-involvement. Back off. Lower their importance to you. They have come to cast such a big shadow in your life that you cannot see God. They are in the way. Get them out from between you and God. Otherwise you will make an idol of them in your inability to relate to God because of them. You have put them in God's place. Joseph's brothers were this agitated about what Joseph thought of them. He said to them, "Do not be afraid! Am I in the place of God?" (Genesis 50:19). It took some backing off for them to perceive differently the man whom they hated enough to sell into slavery. He was not a tyrant but a person who was trying to help them keep alive. Their loss of perspective, their poor judgment, and their confusion had to be changed. Quietness in their noisy hearts called for their backing off from their obsessive fear of their brother's power to hurt them. You may fear that people in your arena of living are there to hurt you. Do not be afraid of them. Do not put them in God's place. Back off from your over-involvement with them.

Turning Aside

Another remarkably quieting discipline to bring silence into your fretful being is turning aside from the turbulent stream of life to one of the quieter pools that catch your eye. It may not be a pool. It may be a plant, an animal, a child. Moses was in his wilderness, tending to his sheep. He saw a bush burning that did not seem to burn up in the process. He said, "I must turn aside and look at this great sight, and see why the bush is not burned up" (Exodus 3:3). When the Lord saw that he turned aside, he revealed himself to Moses. What if Moses had not turned aside? Elizabeth Barrett Browning comments on this when she says:

> Earth's crammed with heaven,
> And every common bush afire with God;
> But only he who sees, takes off his shoes,
> The rest sit around it and pluck blackberries
> And daub their faces unaware[7]

I saw a wise and considerate minister at his work on an Easter morning. He had finished his sermon and was greeting persons as they filed by. A long line of them were there—persons back for the Easter holidays after having moved away, persons home from college, persons with special greetings for him, persons wanting to be near a man who had been through severe griefs with them during the year prior to Easter. A seven- or eight-year-old girl broke through the line and dashed to him. She pulled at his sleeve and asked to whisper in his ear. He turned aside from the long line, dropped down to ear level with her, and listened intently to what she had to say. She took a little while. To him it was as if there were no other persons in the place except her. The rest of the waiting line began to shift from one foot to another somewhat impatiently. Yet this pastor turned aside from them and gave this child his fullest attention. To me, this was a pageant of serenity, quietness of heart, and decisiveness of action.

Breaking Out

One of the monotonous, whirring noises in your heart is the plod-ding routine of your accustomed role and duties. The closer to these tasks and functions you get, the more enclosed you feel by the unremitting noise of routine. Similarly, you have functioned in the title and position that you have so that your very selfhood begins and ends with that title and the institution that surrounds it. The rack-ets, clatterings, bangings, and screamings directed at that institution are indistinguishable from your very self. This is being in prison unawares. There is no prison so effective as that in which the impris-oned ones have no awareness of their bondage.

Breaking out of such bondage creates all sorts of dismay, misun-derstanding, and sometimes outright rejection. How could you do such a thing? That is a good question. Moses must have had some-thing of that experience when he left Egypt. He did not endear him-self to the Pharaoh by violently killing one of the slavemasters who was unjust to the Israelites. The Pharaoh sought to kill him. He broke out of his role and identity with the Egyptians. He fled to the wilderness of Midian. How could he do such a thing?

That is a good question. Moses must have had something of that experience when he left Egypt. He did not endear himself to the Pharaoh by violently killing one of the slavemasters who was unjust to the Israelites. The Pharaoh sought to kill him. He broke out of his role and identity with the Egyptians. He fled to the wilderness of Midian. How could he do such a thing?

Your old acquaintances—not friends—will think of you as almost having died if you break out of your accustomed way of doing things, if you decide that their ways are no longer yours. You will experience unasked-for loneliness, which becomes a prelude to the privacy and solitude that you need for the kind of silence that will heal your noisy heart. That silence will enable you to think new thoughts. You will develop green growing edges to a new being you vaguely sense you are becoming as you break out of your old routine.

Morton Kelsey tells a story about St. Teresa:

> One day, trying to become still in the chapel, the saint
> noticed that the altar hangings were crooked. "How
> careless the sacristan is," she said to herself. "I must. . . .
> No. I am here to pray, not to tell the sacristan what to
> do." With a smile she quieted down, only to hear a sharp
> noise on the roof where some tiles were being replaced.
> "That careless workman!" she thought. "I had better get
> out of here. No mere man could do it right. . . . No, not
> now," and once more, she returned to rebuild silence.[8]

Teresa broke out of her role as the "manager" of mere men and
her routine of seeing to it that things were done perfectly. Building
and rebuilding silence called into action her higher vocation—to give
herself to the silence in which her noisy heart would be made new by
the indwelling presence of God.

The response to life is serenity in the face of noise. That calls for
breaking out of roles and responding to the calling to silence and to
God's work in progress within us making all things new. The new
vocation is to becoming the new being into which you are being
made by God.

chapter three

DOWN-TO-EARTH

CENTERING

IN SILENCE

The meditation many people do certainly is not transcendental. You probably do not claim to think "outside" or "above" this world. You are probably more interested in down-to-earth concerns. I am. The spume of the flow of events around me is so evident and so fast that I simply do not connect up with most of the things I read about meditation, the things that full time "meditators" talk about.

You may be one of the millions who have also decided to find and nurture silence in the middle of a noisy world. I am with you. That is the way silence grows most often with me. So, let's look at some specific ways in which you can go about this nurturing process in such an environment.

Nurturing silence in the noisy heart calls for a frank reassessment of that noisy environment in which you live. The whole process of doing so can be called down-to-earth centering.

Down-to-Earth Centering

By this term I mean that you value silence as the collecting point of your whole being. You concentrate upon silence as a basis of choice for your day's activities (to the limit of your opportunities). You hunt for silence as the center or focus of your external as well as your inner arena of life. You rest upon silence. You gather your life about it as a center. You do not necessarily go to a monastery. You do not break away from the sweaty existence that other people live. You do not ordinarily find a mountain onto which to retreat. You probably do not reach for exotic forms of new or old religion to be your "silence fad." On the contrary, you stick with the earthy existence you have been dealt. The action situation in which you are living now is the scene of your silence. You begin there to nurture silence on behalf of your noisy heart.

You may or may not be a part of a community of other persons who join you in this in the days work. In any case, the group of you are not separatists. You are in the thick of things side by side with them in noisy activities. Yet as a group you have a kinship with each other in a sort of brotherhood and sisterhood of the common life. You are in the world, but you have chosen a different center for your life than the way of conflicts noise, chatter, uproar, and idle gossip. You turn a deaf ear to the untested and unexamined statements people repeat as if they were all true simply because someone said that they were. You do not engage in marathon filibusters to get your own way. You avoid deliberate hassles to intimidate others. You do not impatiently wait until others get through talking so that you can say what you have been preparing to say while they are talking.

You have chosen a way of life that concentrates upon silence. You focus on listening. You value the cost of paying attention not only to what other persons say but also to what you yourself say. You weigh and wait for the right thing to say before speaking. You have listened to your own emotions as indicators of what other persons are actually going through. Your feelings are barometers for measuring your empathy for what they are experiencing. Consequently you perceive other people more reflectively and accurately. You respond to them in a more considered and considerate way. Of course, you may frustrate and aggravate other people in the process. They are accustomed to an immediate answer without such centering of the self, such aiming of one's words, such quieting of the heart to hear one's innermost feelings before shaping words around them. As I describe your down-to-earth centering, I recall sitting in a counseling session with a young Quaker student at Earlham School of Religion in Richmond, Indiana. He started to say something and then caught himself: "Forgive me. Did I interrupt your train of thought?" I was amazed at such considerateness.

Internally, centering means that you silence the contending opinions you have within your heart. You do not feel one way about any one thing or one person. You may feel many ways. You do your best to call a halt to these noisy crosscurrents of personal feelings, opinions, and ideas. You start over. You center upon that person's own deepest need. You try to identify what his or her needs are. You center upon what God's estimate of this person was in creation and is now in God's redemptive wisdom and love. You struggle to identify that person's uniqueness. Thomas Merton quotes Eric Gill as saying, "The artist is not a special kind of man, but every man is a special kind of artist."[1] If you are struggling with a great decision about the way you spend your life, then what is your uniqueness and your special artistry? In what ways are you most completely you and not someone else?

Centering now becomes the discovery of God's image within you. You are standing in awe in that totally silent inner sanctum of your very self. Merton again expresses it best:

> At the center of our being is a point of nothingness which is untouched by sin and illusion, a point of pure truth, a point or spark which belongs to God, which is never at our disposal, from which God disposes of our lives, which is inaccessible to the fantasies of our own mind or brutalities of our own will. This little point of . . . *absolute poverty* is the pure glory of God in us. It is so to speak God's name written in us, as our poverty, as our indigence, as our dependence, as our sonship. It is like a pure diamond, blazing with the invisible light of heaven. It is in everybody, and if we could see it we would see these billions of points of light coming

together in the face and blaze of a sun that would make
all the darkness and cruelty of life vanish completely. . . .
I have no program for this seeing. It is only given. But
the gate of heaven is everywhere.[2]

I am glad he does not have a program for seeing this. Programs
produce much of the darkness and cruelty of which he speaks. From
these come the noise of solemn assembly, the summit conferences,
the power struggles, the pomp and circumstance, and the poignant
need for the very vision of each other that Merton prescribes. I prefer to stick with the unprogrammed way. Yet, just because a way is
unprogrammed does not mean that you do not choose a way of centering. To the contrary, you choose to center down, and that makes
all the difference. The discovery of "the pure glory of God" in you
becomes the basis for the discovery of it in the people around you,
causing the growth not of a program but of a way of life. That makes
all the difference. As with Robert Frost, so with you and me:

Two roads diverged in a wood, and I—
I took the one less traveled by,
And that has made all the difference.[3]

Centering down, then, is not a program but a choosing.
Centering down is a discipline for every hour, every day, every week,
every event of your life. The "road taken" is more than just poetry. It
is a discipline of life. It is very practical.

Unloading the Sensory Overload

All around you every day, someone is demanding your attention with
loud noises of the eye and ear, which may or may not be sounds. Yet
they are immediately translated by your brain into sounds. The cues
at the bottom of a television picture, warning you of an approaching
tornado, speak louder than any words or music coming from the
tube. Musician Paul Simon writes of the sound of silence. Thomas
Merton, Paul Simon, you, and I may not have a program, but the

people bowing and praying to their neon god in Paul Simon's famous song definitely have a program—advertisement.

In my city there is one particular highway which is, continuously, neon sign upon neon sign. The street is one of the busiest and most dangerous thoroughfares in our state. Yet when I want to go to the city toward which it leads, I do not have to choose to go that way. I can go another way that leads through quiet villages, through uncluttered rural roads, forests, open fields, and areas free of neon clutter and clamor for my attention. I get there just as soon. I can experience a sound of silence unpunctuated by neon signs. The road taken does make all the difference.

Another choice my wife and I discovered on a journey to Quebec, Canada. Rather than travel in August or July, the peak tourist season, we chose to travel in October. Rather than travel by the heavily populated freeways, we chose the old roads, which are now little used. We found the traffic much lighter, the signs fewer, the prices for everything lower, and the population in much less of a hurry. We stuck to the 55-mile-per-hour speed limit and were less likely to be tailgated by other motorists. We did not have to play alternate passing and being passed by trucks whose drivers were trying to even the speed limit by speeding down hills and laboring up hills. Taking the old road was less hazardous. Fewer signs reached higher and higher into the sky to capture our attention and to interrupt the sounds of silence we enjoyed as we observed farms, vineyards, cattle, farmers plowing with horses and mules and not huge tractors. We actually saw one person just sitting and thinking!

Finding Pockets of Silence in the Day's Work

During your day you will be hard pressed to find silence on the job, particularly if you work in a large city, a large industry, a large business. The nearest thing to a place of quietness many people find is in the restroom. A place of work can easily be portrayed as a place where people talk without speaking and hear without listening.

If you are committed to nurturing silence, you will measure your day in terms of that commitment. For example, you may choose some day to eat your lunch alone in your office, behind a stack of boxes in a warehouse, or in a little-used park near your place of work. You may use your coffee break to go for a walk. You stop by the water fountain only to rehydrate yourself. I discovered that a long brisk walk to lunch on the main street of my city away from our hospital teaching clinic gave me exercise, freed me of seeing many people I had to talk with or listen to, and gave me a time to let my soul catch up with my body.

I can recall how the massive noise of a cotton mill shut out all conversation. We had to learn how to read lips, to make signs and signals of communication with our hands, head, and feet. Yet the massive noise was an overcast for all other noises and I experienced profound times of inner quietness in my own heart. I felt the growth of a mystical consciousness start in my life at that time. In my hospital work, I wondered why on earth the hospital had installed a music speaker into my office. I now know that it was to create an overcast of pleasant sound to maintain a degree of privacy from voices through thin walls. Personally, I prefer to have walls that are sound insulated. It was difficult for me to function with that music going.

The present group of younger persons are accustomed to television and radio going while they are working. They do not live comfortably with the sounds of silence. I certainly am not putting them down for this. They have their own lifestyle. Possibly the music covers out all other noises and enables them to commune within as the machine noises in the cotton mills did for me when I was young.

Centering Upon the World of No Words

Another breakthrough occurs when you realize, in the quiet environment which you create, that the most important part of your world is not expressed in words. The word is heard. It needs to be heard as well as spoken clearly to mean what it says. Much noise in our hearts results from the confusion created between what is said and what is meant with words. John Woolman, the early American Quaker (1720-72), told of visiting among the Native Americans in Pennsylvania. They did not understand English, and he did not understand their language. Interpreters had great trouble in translating. Woolman decided to shift from direct conversation with them to prayer in conversation with God. This he did, and the meeting ended with his prayer that if he had prayed aright, the expression of Divine love would come through beyond his words. After the meeting he noted that one of the Native Americans, who was filled with concern about the well-being of his people, was speaking to one of the interpreters. Woolman was told that he had said, "I love to hear where words come from."[4]

Words come from the realm of silence. Alfred Korzybski, a leading scientist of semantics (the meaningful use of words), says that significant understanding of the way things really are cannot be expressed in words:

> We must have *other means* to indicate this difference. We
> must show with our hand, by pointing with our finger
> to an object, and by being silent outwardly as well as
> inwardly, which silence we may indicate by closing our
> lips with the other hand. . . . On this last level we can
> look, handle, but must be silent.[5]

At the positive level, then, meaning and understanding come from the depths of silence, and, as Albert Einstein said of his own thought processes, most of his basic thoughts were "visual and some of muscular type. Conventional words and other signs have to be sought for laboriously only in a secondary stage."[6]

The tragic source of noise in our hearts is the way in which words confuse, hide, distort, and raise shrillness. Words can alienate people from each other, set misunderstandings into concrete that only blasting and drilling can remove, and make it impossible for some people ever to be reconciled and properly related. Ruth Deich and Patricia Hodges encounter these negative levels of words in their work with brain-damaged and mentally challenged children learning to speak without the use of speech but through touch, sight, and a relationship with a patient teacher: "Language can even be, and has been, used in negative ways in order to lie, or to cover truth with irrelevancies. Every day the various news media give ample evidence of obfuscation, lies couched in bureaucratic jargon, and propaganda spewed out by dictators and non-dictators alike."[7]

All this is true. At the same time, language or words are one of our major means of coping with life. However, survival values are at stake when words become a barrier of noise in the human heart. The capacity to cope also involves the cultivation of the wordless silence that is primary to productive human thought and direct contact with God. Words become flesh in order to be clear and unmistakable. Nurturing silence in the noisy heart calls for a radical shift from the use of the sense of hearing alone to the use of all the senses in becoming alive to the quiet ones of the world. Before this can happen, however, such a major shift involves some rarely used disciplines.

Getting Over the Need to Have the First and Last Words

You may compete with your parents, teachers, pastors, and other leaders in your life (while they compete with each other) in doing something they have never done before and in which you will be a "first." In doing so, you may react so far against all that they have ever deposited in your heart that you will be beset with a battle, rejecting everything they ever taught you. The noise this battle creates overcasts everything you say or do. Before that, in the quiet confines of your own heart, this battle rages in your deepest sources of thinking. It may come between you and the silence of God, which speaks louder than words. You may not even be able to perceive God accurately because of it. An example of this is the poem I received permission from an eighteen-year-old woman to share with you:

> She always wanted them to love her
> But they did not even like her
> She pretended she did not care
> And no one knew except her and
> God
> But God loved her
> At night God talked to her

And made her feel good and warm inside
Like somebody special

One day she asked them
To love her, a little
Like all good parents did then.
They looked down at her
"You are a Dumb Little Kid," they said,
"Why can't you be like your brother?
He doesn't bother us."

After that she felt like a Dumb
Little Kid
She felt like a bother
And she stopped feeling good and warm inside
Like somebody special

And she buried God in the ground
With a weedy dandelion in the
Dirt
Next to the grave.

—Kim

The tragedy is that she wants to have the last word, not only in the argument with her parents but also with God. Somewhere, somehow, the parents also want to have the last word with her. Such battles have been known to go on throughout the lives of families.

Sometime, some place, a cease-fire has to be declared. A willingness to let someone else have the last word—as if it matters. A kind of mellowing forgiveness takes place.

Parents are nonnegotiable. We cannot send them back and get a refund. We cannot exchange them for someone else. We do not even have a warranty that requires them to be repaired to our specifications. Isn't life too short to let it be dominated by the racket of such word battles?

Similarly, husbands and wives often talk their marriage into an early grave as they compete for the first and last words. Obviously communication is important in a marriage, but wordless communication tends to be deepest, requires the most trust, and demands the most considerateness. Listening with all the senses and not just the ears—to tones, inflections, glances, touches, deeds, distances, closenesses, smells, tastes, rituals, and changes of rituals—is the nonverbal source of wise love in a marriage. Judging each other by what one means and where the words come from is a source of serenity and the calming of noisy hearts in a home.

At work also, the battle rages for who scooped the other, who had the first word, who started which program, whose original idea it was in the first place. When controversy arises within a staff, long meetings are based on the assumption that someone will find just the exact word to say—the bowknot on the packaged problem. Having the final word, even if it is a perfect squelch, is the order of the day. It's also the source of noises in the hearts of staff members when they go home at night and rehearse what they wish they had said. What pain it is to think of the right thing to say twenty-four hours too late!

When all is said and done, the critical issue in power struggles is who's going to have the final say. However, if a group agrees that each does not have to have the final say, then the consensus of every person's best interest has at least a chance of becoming central. Apart from some such coming to terms with the noise created by human pride in the human heart, the members of the group tend to withdraw from each other, either in factions or in resignations.

Let me share my own feelings about such a hassle:

> And they said to me, "Go to, now—let's have a fight."
> And I said to them, "But what are we fighting about
> and what are we fighting for?" But I heard only a
> buzzing among them. A few giggles.

> So I went away and climbed a great hill and looked at
> the blinking neon signs across a great river on which
> hovered the commerce of nations.

> Out of the silence I heard the Wisdom of God: "Do you want to know what the fighting is for? I will tell you: two yards of sackcloth, a bucket of ashes, and a quart of gall. The sackcloth and ashes will be to those who can still feel enough after the fight to sense its futility and repent. The quart of gall will be for those who can no longer feel, either for themselves or for others, and can only taste that which is bitter."

Getting over the need for the first and last word is a rarely used discipline, but it is the royal road to silence in a noisy heart.

Listening with Full Attention and All Five Senses

You swell with speech unuttered, and silence after silence strangles your voice when you try to put into words the deepest matters of life and death that concern you. What can you say when your closest friend has lost his or her spouse? What do you say when you see your wife after both of you have learned that the child to whom she has just given birth was born dead? What do you say when you have seen years of work go into nothingness as your business has been declared bankrupt? In a more specific sense, how can a combat veteran of innumerable battles possibly tell you what it was like? If you are a nurse, a physician, a social worker with migrant poor, a pastor who conducts funerals and weddings on the same day, how can you put into words the mixed emotions you feel about the day's work? All have been filled with such an unutterably tragic sense of life. We feel the shortness of life, the unfairness, the certainty of inescapable laws of life and death. Yet the mystery cannot be put into words. The tragic sense of life is carried as a wistful silence.

Yet a deeper thing happens. We also develop a sharper awareness of the beauties of life, a keener sensitivity to using our other senses in addition to hearing. We learn with Miguel Unamuno, "God is simply the Love that springs from universal suffering and becomes consciousness."[8] We learn with the psalmist of the God who speaks but is not heard:

> The heavens are telling the glory of God;
>> and the firmament proclaims his handiwork.
> Day to day pours forth speech,
>> and night to night declares knowledge.
> There is no speech, nor are there words;
>> their voice is not heard;
> yet their voice goes out through all the earth,
>> and their words to the end of the world. [Psalm 19:1-4]

By coming into direct contact in the depths of silence with such a God, we become alive to a way of seeing God through a quiet heart that has been refined through fires of adversity.

And we develop an additional discipline: the power to listen with all our senses. We listen to God's silent word in the very bodies and behaviors of ourselves and the persons around us who may even be total strangers:

> I see something of God each hour of the twenty-four,
>> and each moment then,
> In the faces of men and women I see God, and in my
>> own face in the glass,
> I find letters from God dropt in the street, and every one
>> is sign'd by God's name,
> And I leave them where they are, for I know that
>> wheresoe'er I go,
> Others will punctually come for ever and ever.[9]

Take a look at some specifics of a few things you can listen for with all of your senses, including hearing:

Note the sense of coolness that comes over you upon entering an air-conditioned room after sweaty work in the sun, in an unair-conditioned ward in a charity hospital, in a steel-mill smelting room, or the sticky-wet air conditioning of a wears shop.

Appreciate the feeling of worth that comes when someone you love dries the sweat from your brow while you are digging, when you are sick, or after you have been weeping.

Remember being out of breath from laughter at something hilariously funny.

Do not overlook the sudden feeling of detachment that you sense when you are in a large shopping center and note the vast difference in the kinds of things that people of different stations in life are buying.

Make note of a child who is lost from his or her parents and tugs at your sleeve thinking that's who you are. Then the child realizes you are not . . . and is frightened of you as a stranger. You are pressed to communicate care and friendship without overstepping the edges of your strangeness. You don't just stand there. You drop to your knees. You keep your distance. You look the child in the face so that he or she does not have to bend the neck backward to see you. You wait for the child not to run from you. You smile. You suddenly are not just a stranger but also a friend.

Or, you are walking through a crowded room. You suddenly feel that someone is watching you. You look around. Someone is watching you. A child is sucking on a bottle, cuddled in a woman's arms. The child (Is it a boy or a girl? It's hard to tell from here. Is it dressed in blue or pink?) is tracking you with its eyes while it hangs on to every swig of its milk. You smile. You wave. The child stops sucking the bottle long enough to smile back. You are renewed.

Then, too, you get messages from God from the bodies of persons who are unaware that you are seeing them. This person's hands are gnarled, drawn, and trembly from arthritis. That person's hands are smooth and well kept, relaxed and silently resting in the lap. Another person's hands have coffee-colored spots that let you know the years are passing. Yet another person's hands are clenched but there is nothing in them. What is he angry about? Of what is she afraid? God is speaking to you in the harassed helplessness of such hands as these. The shaken finger of a protesting person who has just been referred to somebody else to whom they will hear a retelling of their story again teaches you one source of violent anger. Do you plan to be the one who chooses to be where the buck stops and deal with the problem yourself rather than refer it? These persons may be messengers from God.

Zoroastrianism calls such persons "angels." The Old Testament depicts persons we do not know and yet with whom we struggle as "angels of the Lord." When you find yourself struggling with a total stranger, be careful. God may be trying to get a message about your noisy heart through to you by way of this stranger. The New Testament puts it this way: "Do not neglect to show hospitality to strangers, for by doing that some have entertained angels without knowing it" (Hebrews 13:2). Slow down. Listen intently. Center your attention on the wordless meanings of this fretful stranger. Break out of your mold. Even the most untutored person senses whether you speak from your own quiet heart, or simply convey the noises you have been told to say.

Centering Down in a Silent Evening at Home

Now the day is over. You go home. The hands of a child trace the rims of your glasses. The hands of a lover trace the dimple in your cheek or the wrinkles on your forehead. The hands of a guest are extended to you in warm greeting. The hands of a next-door neighbor bring you a dish that was lovingly prepared so that, even though words will not say the right thing at a time of grief or celebration, a well-prepared dish of food will say it.

Your mate then, after thanking and bidding good-bye to the neighbor, places the food on the table. You let your mate know you are a partner by helping put dishes and silverware in place. You eat together in silence. Is it a friendly silence? Is it a warm silence? Is it a bored silenced Is it a sullen, angry silence? Is it a reverent silence? Is it a gentle silence? Do you touch each other? What does it mean? These silences come between whatever is actually said. They are freighted with meaning, and you and I fool ourselves if we say that we do not translate them into noises or music in our hearts.

The meal is finished. Each of you arises, takes your dishes to the sink, scrapes them for washing and joins in cleaning up the eating area. But you are interrupted and must answer the telephone. The unseen person is pouring out a story. You are called upon to give undivided attention, listening at its height. You say little or nothing. You may not be able to do what is requested of you. You may suggest what, to you, is a better idea. You listen. You hear the caller out. Your arm holding the telephone lets you know how much time has passed. Why did the person find it easier to talk with you on the telephone than looking, right at you? Maybe you cannot listen with your eyes. But, then again, you hear the undertones and overtones of the voice more clearly over the telephone.

The telephone is now a threat to the silence you have earned after a day's work in a noisy world. After listening to another's problems, you struggle with the need to call a colleague friend, instantly replaying the skirmishes, battles, and frustrations of your day. Resist it with your whole being! Turn the telephone off. Unplug the jack. If you don't have that kind of telephone, invest in one. As a mini retreat, don't make any telephone calls except in the toughest of emergencies in the evening.

Now that you have silenced the telephone, you must face the television. Everyone is trying to get into your private quarters at prime time. And prime time, for the person concerned with centering a noisy heart upon silence, demands forms of resistance to television. Just listen to the amount of screaming and shouting that characters do in the situation comedies. Soap operas—interestingly in contrast—are filled with soft voices and quiet seriousness about pseudo-adult concerns. In violent contrast to both of these is the murderous misuse of the automobile in the whodunits. Handguns and rifles come in for their fair share of the violence, but the front runner in violence, noise, and chaos is the automobile. A steady diet of listening and watching these three kinds of material is one sure way to nurture noise in a noisy heart.

However, television is not all this way. The measuring line I suggest for television: choose, ahead of time, the presentations that will create reflective conversation between family members. Also, I suggest other patterns than television viewing for making the evening a time for nurturing silence in a noisy heart.

Debriefing vs. Rehashing

Nurture silence in the evening by avoiding the fretful rehash of the day's work to your family members, your roommates, or friends. Debriefing with these intimates is an important part of the mutual ties that bind you together. But this should be confined to an hour or less. Otherwise, it can become a driven, repetitive churning over of the same problems for a whole evening, causing you to go to bed ajangle with the noise and chatter of the day.

Talk it through, but don't filibuster! Then relax and let silence settle down over your restless spirit, still raw and hurting from the stresses of the day.

The Twelve-Hour Silence

I remember one home near Stroudsburg, Pennsylvania, which I visited for a week. Quakers Bob and Edith Platt were my hosts. They observed what Quakers call "the compline." This means that from eight p.m. to eight a.m. no one spoke at all. I shared in this fellowship of silence.

At first, it nearly panicked me. I was accustomed to being talked to, with, and at until eleven or twelve in the evening. Not so at Bob and Edith Platt's home. Gradually I began to become soaked in silence. I could reorder the jumbled events of the day as surely in silence as Edith put the much-used home in order.

Such a pattern, if instituted at our house, would do several things. Maybe you would find them happening at yours. A compline would keep us from unduly rehashing the battles and bothers of the day. Second, it would mean that we would not take or make telephone calls after eight o'clock in the evening. Third, it would probably push us into reading more significantly each day. Fourth, it would enrich the wordless touching, seeing, hearing, smiling, holding, and kissing that goes on between family members. More no-word signals of affection would emerge. Fifth, it would stimulate the awareness of the Spirit of God who "intercedes for us with sighs too deep for words." Prayer would be less wordy and more serious. Finally, we would probably sleep much better. Our dreams would be satisfaction dreams instead of frustration dreams.

Yet the compline idea is not practical for most of us, not in its entirety. Nevertheless, you can learn from it the difference between debriefing the days activities and rehashing again and again things about which you are anxious. You can also use this discipline of the spirit to mend your noisy hearts of calling others and allowing them to usurp your evenings with long-winded telephone conversations. You can also shift to more wordless forms of communication and allow time for contemplation in the home at night.

Sleep and Silence in Your Noisy Heart

Don't rebuke yourself if you cannot sleep. Instead, ask yourself: "What unmade decisions keep me anxious?" You may be able to make a decision as to what to do.

In Jesus' parable of the Prodigal Son, the son says, "I will get up and go to my father, and I will say to him . . ." (Luke 15:18). If he arose, he may have been lying awake—sleepless. We do not know. We do know that troubled relationships will keep you awake and that they call for decisive action.

You may not be able to decide now. You need more facts, more time, or you need something else to happen. If you cannot decide now, you can decide when you can decide. That quiets your noisy, indecisive heart and prepares you for sleep.

You may be too tired to sleep. You hurt all over from fatigue. You may need to rest as a prelude to sleep. Just lie quietly and breathe deeply. If you sleep with someone, and that person is asleep, then get your breathing in step with theirs. This rests you as a prelude to sleep. If your thoughts are racing, shift them to a series of pleasant memories that continue to renew you even now. Views of special persons and places you enjoyed earlier, events that made life better for you, and thoughts you have used to help others are all available to you in your own memory. Before you know it you are asleep.

chapter four

SILENCING

THE STRANGE NOISES

WITHIN YOUR HEART

Within this earthly temple, there is a crowd.
There is one of me that is humble;
And there is one of me that is proud.
There is one of me that loves his neighbor as himself;
And there is one of me that loves naught but fame and pelf.
There is one of me that is repentant for his sins;
And there is one of me that unrepentant sits and grins.
From much undue noise of heart I would be free,
If I could once decide which is me.

The crowd within you and me that we call "myself" is a noisy
bunch. The above verse is of unknown origin. It concentrates on
the good and bad noises within your heart. You have become accustomed to these noises. They prompt you to do this and not
to do that.

However, the unknown author does not mention the strange,
unfamiliar, and unknown noises within your heart. These are spooky
and frightening noises. Everything about these noises is foreign,
strange, and alien to who you think you are in even the worst

estimates of yourself. They prompt nameless dread, making you uneasy—about what, you cannot put into words. You are both mystified and fascinated by these noises. Yet you move along your daily pursuits. You are aware of the presence of these noises in dreams; in half-walking and half-sleeping states; and when you are exceedingly tired, yet have to keep on functioning. You sense these internally strange but vaguely familiar noises as if they were from a movie that you have seen before but just cannot get the sequence straight. In other words, your life begins to feel like a rerun that was unpleasant in the first place.

Skeletons of Unhappiness and Happiness

You can get acquainted with these strange noises. You can silence them by courageously removing their strangeness. Some will disappear. Others become quiet, serene, and friendly noises. You need a clear range of vision. You need someone to introduce you to them. May I try?

Think of these noises the way you would of your skeleton. I recall very well visiting Caulfield's Novelty Shop in our town with our youngest son when he was about four years old. It was a cool October Saturday just before Halloween, and we were looking for a Halloween costume for him. In the show window, as we looked at the different costumes, we also saw a "for-real" skeleton of a human body. Charles asked, "What's that?" I began to explain that all of us have a skeleton within to hold our bodies together and enable us to stand up, walk, and do all the things we do. He said, "You mean I have one of those things inside me?" I said, "Yes." He shook himself, drew his body into a knot, hugged himself with his own arms, and said, "Brrrrr! That scares me!"

It seemed strange to him that such an "out of this world"-looking thing would be a necessary part of his insides. You may feel the same way about strange spiritual sounds within yourself. It takes nerve to make friends with a skeleton. Years later, Charles became a medical student who learned the names of each bone in the skeleton of a cadaver.

However, the skeleton experience can be a parable for describing the less literal skeletons within you. They rattle automatically; you assume that this strange innerness is bad, dark, evil. Such a thing could not be good. It makes you distinctly uncomfortable and therefore must be all wrong. It is as if you are working away at a task in your own home and suddenly look up to a person whom you vaguely recognize but do not know. You are frightened.

I can identify with that. I came home one afternoon and my wife and our neighbors were gathered in our kitchen. The house had been broken into and robbed in our absence. The thief had stolen the usual things—television, radios, silverware, a fur-collared coat—anything that would sell quickly. The losses were not as great as the feeling of terror, uneasiness, and tension when we asked, "What if one or both of us had been here when the person broke and entered? How would we have dealt with this intruder into our home?" He was a stranger, but he was here to do us harm. How would we deal with someone like that? You can only speculate.

Yet, this feeling that strange sounds are, by definition, evil is the most natural first reaction you may be having at the thoughts I am introducing to you here. Arnold Toynbee said that we are terrified by our own solitude. However, this fear of the unknown and the strange takes a new turn of creative inner peace, quieting noisy heart, in the words of a person who wrote to me recently:

> I found the trip into my own mind challenging and ultimately enjoyable. I sometimes think we would do most anything not to travel into our own thoughts. Before I took that trip, I imagined I would find nothing of value, and worse, I would find horrid and fearful monsters there. I spent some time with a psychologist and in one of our first talks I warned him that he was in for a glimpse of something ugly. I looked upon him as a human garbage can, receiving the putrid rot of a human mind. Many of the fears, guilty and pent-up frustrations were not pleasant; but I found a strength, an endurance, and a will: to be whole and happy. Once

> I realized that there is good in my heart, I took it one
> step further and acknowledged that there is good in all
> minds.... That was the skeleton of my happiness; now to
> put muscle on that skeleton.

The skeleton within you can indeed be the "skeleton of your happiness." It need not be anything other than it is: a real honest-to-goodness part of your best self, a frame for putting on muscle for energetic enjoyment of life. You were created to listen without undue fear to the strange noises within you. What you learn about yourself from these noises can be put into action in your behalf. Otherwise, the noise, the banging, the break-ins, the frightenings will needlessly continue. You can change that now. Specific ways are available for moving deeply into the noisy center of your being and getting acquainted with these strange noises.

Meet the Strange Noises from Your Past

Many of these strange noises are really a very primitive part of you. You rather early found a part of your surroundings in life to be something you definitely did not like. You were repelled by it. You recoiled. You may have seen the treadmill way of life lived by your family of origin—your parents, brothers, sisters, uncles, aunts, and cousins. They took for granted the kind of work they were doing, the kind of values they cherished, the kind of hopes they were willing to settle for, and the way they used their minds and time. None of them ever considered, except in their dreams and imaginations, that there might be a different and even better way of life. They had no ambition to free themselves from the closed-in surroundings of the small town, the mill village, the mining community, the farm, the ghetto. They felt themselves fated to be like this.

You loved them. You wanted them to have a better way of life. You wanted them to be ambitious like you were. You urged them to join you in your own ambitions for a good education, a larger world of interests, a freedom from slavery to an industrial or agricultural system that used people up in their bodily health and strength but provided no nurture for their mental and spiritual growth. Much to your surprise, they rejected you. They made fun of you and all your ideas, They insisted on being "common folk," whereas you felt that they were more common than folk. So you became the oddball. You launched out on your own without their blessing. You left them behind, feeling yourself a stranger to them. Thus, you could grow and survive even if they did not want to do so with you.

Years passed. Their words and instructions became strange to you. They are your blood kin, but you have met people who are more nearly your brothers and sisters, father and mother than they are. What a cruel fate! Why could they not have shared your life with you?

Whatever else you say, however, their way of life is not your way of life. They are not you. Yet they and what they represent are, in fact, a very real part of your heart. The sounds they make in your memory disturb you.

What could you have done but cut yourself off from them, if you were going to be yourself? Nothing. It is one of those ironies of fate. All well and good. But the whole thing leaves you uneasy. Those experiences that were yours, when you consider them—ten, twenty, or thirty years later—seem as if they had happened to someone else. What a set of strange feelings they are! They echo in your heart as the noisy memories of your past. You may hear these strange noises only in your sleep, when you dream of things that happened long ago and far away. Upon awakening, you feel as if you have wrestled with a stranger, so foreign is your dream to anything you now know or do. You think few people around would understand if you talked with them about this. You can get along very well as long as you are in the role that you have earned for yourself the hard way. There, you are in control of things. However, when you are alone, when you are weary, and when you try to get into a place of solitude, you hear the noises of the past. No wonder your noisy heart fears silence!

Or your experience may be the reverse of this: You come from a background of great privilege, sophistication, and public trust. You have highly successful parents. Your brothers and sisters are high achievers in the worlds of the verbal, of status symbols, of ideas, of doing things in a proper and dignified manner. Very early you became uncomfortable with all this. You preferred to dress differently, to think differently, to use a very simple but blunt vocabulary. No college-professional route for your life! Rather, you chose to learn from direct experience. You were not a sit-at-home-and-talk kind. Abstractions were for persons who had little or no sense of life as it is really lived. You prefer to work with your hands. You do rather than say things.

Your parents used all their influence and money to "smooth the way" for you. You needed their help, yet you resented it. After a while—and it took you longer because you insisted on learning from direct experience rather than books, earning your way on personal merit rather than on diplomas, degrees, and certificates—your own native intelligence had its way. You became a self-made person after your own intuitive design. In fact, you probably did it the same way your father or mother did. You began to win in life. You were born, but not to lose. You were born to be you. Being you just took a little longer and was certainly an unpaved road to travel.

But still the strange noises within you make you uneasy. Are you not really more like your parents than you are different?

Nevertheless, you avoid being still or quiet. You can't stand silence. When you become completely relaxed and quiet, you, too, begin to hear the strange noises within. You are awkward, uncomfortable, ill at ease. How on earth did a person like you become part of such a family as this? Why is it that you do not seem to have their blessing nor are able to give them yours?

Another reader may feel the strange vibrations within in a different way. Your parents, brothers and sisters, aunts, uncles, cousins, were all very religious people. They were big churchgoers, doers, and speakers. You were constantly being pushed into the limelight of their religiosity. You got a bellyful of this. You decided that such stuff was not you. The strange noises were their noise. You had to be yourself, but before that, you unwittingly decided they would be foreign to you. Their ways would not be your ways.

You may have become the agnostic, the atheist, the hard-nosed scientist who believes only what you can see and handle. You see all this religious nonsense as a victory of the irrational over the human mind. Or perhaps you are not all that hostile to religion; you simply consider it strange to your own way of life. It is not you. If you experience a sense of mystery, awe, and wonder, you do so over a test tube, a patient, a telescope, a microscope, and not over a prayer book a revival meeting, or a rosary. That stuff is not you. Yet that "stuff" makes you uneasy when a genuinely intellectual person you know calmly and quietly shares his or her faith in God.

But then again, is that "stuff" you? You feel strange intimations of things you learned in Sunday school, or that your parents pressed home to your thinking as a child. Why do these sounds stir homesickness in you? They return to make you uneasy, uncomfortable, and awkward. Does a sense of "having been here before" come to you when you are in a meeting of other scientists who are saying things and doing things that vaguely pull at you?

I recall a young physician who related such an experience. He was in a workshop for the improvement of medical education and was entranced by the presentations he was hearing. He had queasy feelings as these things happened. He went back to his hotel room three evenings in a row and spent some time alone, trying to process what he was learning. As he did so, it became very evident to him that the strange sense of déjà vu he felt was arising from forgotten and neglected portions of his experience. He remembered that he had learned Jesus' teachings in the Sermon on the Mount when he was in grammar school. In experiencing the new, he had met some of the same truths he had heard from his youth up. He did so in the silence and solitude of his room when the crowd was not around him. As the queasy feelings within him were identified and welcomed as old friends, silence, peace, and inner tranquillity came over his whole being.

You can do at least three things about the strange noises from your past.

First, you can turn back and get reacquainted with your own roots. This is the way to dignity that many African Americans have taken. This turning back is remembering, recalling. Old and New

Testaments urge a healthy memory. We remember the Sabbath because it reminds us of the enslavement of a people in Egypt. We celebrate the Eucharist, the Lord's Supper, in remembrance of the death, burial, and resurrection of Jesus Christ. We remember the leaders who have led us and consider the outcomes of their lives.

Second, you can reassess the contribution that your own family has made to you. How have the human strengths they gave you enabled you to become the person you are? You can begin to get acquainted with these strengths in you which you have, until now, denied. Your early family—if you are like me—gave you certain unearned gifts that have enabled you to become the person you are: stubbornness, independence, willingness to work even when much of the time it is boring, and a sense of wisdom about human nature that is hidden to the sophisticate, born to the manor.

Certain things that your highly verbal family gave you enable you to decipher some of the masked codes of communication that your snob customers use. They enable you to be a leader, to stand out in your group as the natural leader. They deposited within you a concern for persons that now makes you adept at caring for the best interests of your employees. Hyper-religious parents may have shoved a party-line religion at you for breakfast, lunch, and dinner. In doing so, they imbued you with a sense of commitment that sets you apart literally from time-serving, next-best-chance people in your scientific organization. Long after these sunshine patriots are gone to warmer climates, you are there in the twelve inches of snow standing guard and doing that which you have committed yourself to do. Is there not a quality of steadfastness about you that causes people to wonder why you are so "evangelical" about your cause? That "evangelical" commitment is the strange noise that you feel in your heart.

Silence that knocking at the door of your heart. Admit the source of your sense of commitment.

Third, you can open up conversation with your parents, brothers, sisters, and others about your indebtedness to them. You can express gratitude to them. You no longer have to be an alien. This can cause them to feel a great sense of worth. At the same time, you feel a greater sense of peace and quiet in your heart. You do as Goethe suggested:

> What from your father's heritage is lent,
> Earn it anew, to really possess it.[1]

You have, on your own, earned your parents' heritage anew, with the human strength given you by that heritage. To turn back, to reassess, and have face-to-face conversation will cause a struggle in your heart. You will literally wrestle with the strange noises within. You will claim your own heritage as distinctly yours. You may even feel that you need to be renamed as the new person that you are.

I have seen persons do this. They may have gone through their lives until their mature years of thirty, forty, or even fifty carrying a nickname from their childhood. Now, they double back they get their very own real name. They cease to be called Mickey or some other nickname. They become the person they were named at birth. They finally receive a blessing from their own parental heritage. They are enabled to become a blessing to others. You might be interested in following such an experience of Jacob in the Old Testament. After such a struggle, he changed his name to Israel. Read it in chapters 27-34 of Genesis. It is a remarkable story.

Take a New Look at the Persons You Cannot Know Because You Despise Them

Another way of getting acquainted with the strange noises in your heart is to take a new look at the persons you cannot get to know—because you despise them. Deep noises disturb you at the mention of their names. You can say that the person whom you disparage actually sets old these alarms. You cannot get to know that person. How can you become acquainted with someone who disgusts you from the start? You shrink from the person. You are filled with disquietude. The thought of him or her disturbs you. Then you talk with someone to whom you feel akin, and you disparage the person who sets off all these alarms within you.

To despise other people means to downgrade, to low-rate them. You hold them in contempt, sneer at, and despair of them. The bodily sensation that goes with these feelings is nausea. You have heard people say, "He nauseates me," or, "She nearly makes me vomit when I get around her." Granted, my work may have overexposed me to such attitudes in other people and in myself, but one constant prayer of my life is to be delivered from feelings of disgust. Disgust is one of the most unpleasant emotions I know, one with which I don't want to live for more than a day.

You ask "What has disgust, nausea, or despising to do with my getting acquainted with the strange noises that set off alarms in me?" Just this: When you are disgusted with another person, the green-eyed monster of jealousy may be prompting you. You depreciate others whom you would most want to be like because of their place, their skill, their chance, their luck their good fortune. You ask privately, "Why can't I have such things happen to me?" Out-of-control competitive needs prompt your disgust with the so-called winners.

On the other hand, if you are a front-runner in your outfit, do not be surprised if you are the target of disgust. Others throw down their helmets when you win. You become a reflecting mirror of the person many of your colleagues want to be. You will be tempted to knock yourself out trying to win these colleagues' good will. You will try to help them in every way possible—yet they despise you, sneer at you, and speak against you. Someone put it this way: "I do not know why those people despise me. I never did anything to help them!" Yet, you need their approval so badly that you overdo trying to help them. On their side, they interpret your attempts to help as your thinking they are helpless, weak, and inferior to you. You would do them more good by just letting them be in their own strengths while you cheer their successes. If anyone is going to help anyone, ask them to help you. This is, in honor, to defer to them. They see your help as strength and shrink from it, but they see your need of help as weakness in you asking for strength in them.

Furthermore, your despising others locates the source of many strange sounds that make a very noisy heart for you. The apostle Paul said, "If anyone is detected in a transgression, you who have received the Spirit should restore such a one in a spirit of gentleness. Take care that you yourselves are not tempted" (Galatians 6:1). The noises of your disgust echo in your harshness toward others. If this harshness settles down into a permanent way of life, more and more of your heart becomes foreign, strange, and alien to the rest of you. You diminish as a self; the disgust begins to take over your whole being and run the show. Instead of being briefly cynical or bitter, you become a cynic, a person whose lifestyle is one of disgust. You become a sour, dyspeptic, hostile-humored sneer.

Such a way of life can be tested by asking yourself: "Who is it I consider as foreign, strange, and unclean?" You may have large groups of such persons in classes of people all of whom you label with one disparaging name. You are likely to consider such persons common. You have no use for them. From a belief point of view, persons may be greatly different from you. If you are a professional person with a different approach to the practice of law, to the practice of medicine, to the practice of nursing, to the practice of social work, etc., you can collect to yourself all sorts of epithets, disparaging names, or even vulgar slurs. A colleague can become not a person but an incompetent, quack, or hack. Worse than this, a co-worker may be, not a human being but a turkey, jerk, or liar. People of different social classes may become Establishment, palace guards, lackeys, mouthpieces, dissidents, undignified, trash, or worse.

Jesus felt the disgust of Nathanael. To be from Nazareth was to be a nothing. Nathanael said of Jesus, "Can anything good come out of Nazareth?" (John 1:46). When Nathanael met Jesus personally, however, he had a remarkable change of heart. The noises of his stereotypes of Nazarenes were silenced as he met this particular Nazarene.

The apostle Peter had been reared to think of Gentiles as dogs. Throughout his life this way of thinking plagued him. As a practicing Jew, he particularly did not eat with them, nor did he partake of their unholy food. However, in a dramatic meeting with God, with Cornelius (a Roman centurion of the Italian Cohort), and with the strange new sounds of God's Spirit, Peter discovered that God had not made any human being common or unclean. God was and is no respecter of persons. To despise one group of human beings is to do violence both to them and to yourself. How?

First, you become a class-action thinker. You make a judgment about a whole class of people on the basis of your experience with one or two of them. Then you treat them all as if they were like the one or two with whom you have had trouble. Not necessarily so! To do this is to do an injustice to the tenth or twelfth person whom you meet. That person may or may not fit the mold you made from your dealings with the first one or two persons. You never learn this because you have already prejudged him or her on the basis of an older meeting with someone from his or her race, religion, geographical part of the country, etc.

Put the shoe on the other foot. How would you like to have to pay the bill for someone else who incurred the wrath of a person whom you are seeking to please? Then your own basic humanity recognizes that as painful. You silence your own heart long enough to identify and recognize the strange noise of prejudice within you. You have feelings, too. You would not like to be treated that way.

When you become acquainted with your disgust and deal with it head on, the strange noise becomes a source of openness, quietness, and freedom from the clatter of prejudice. You pause in your judgment of the other people on a class action basis. You wait quietly. You let all individuals become persons in their own right. You watch closely their individual track records. You are released from your fear of them, a noise in the heart not to be underestimated. You let each person prove himself or herself. You give each one the kind of chance you would want for yourself. In fact, you may discover the quiet sense of peace that prompts you to appreciate as your own kinsperson someone whom you had disliked.

I recall such an experience of my own. The editor of a certain magazine was, to me, the world's prime example of everything a person should not believe. I read his editorials, and they were horrible. I watched the kinds of things he permitted to be printed. They were worse. I had never met the man himself. If given the chance, I think I would have avoided it. Then, on one occasion, I was thrown with him in a social situation. We sat by each other. It was a situation in which I was supposed to converse with him as an individual. I was guarded, suspicious, and self-protective.

He came on like a blockbuster: "So you are the man who teaches all this stuff about psychology?"

I maintained enough composure simply to say yes, and no more. I just waited.

Then, much to my surprise, he said, "Great! I am glad. Let me tell you something that means a lot to me. When I was a child, and until I was nineteen years of age, I was a chronic stutterer. I went to a psychologist who helped me overcome my stuttering. He taught me to help other people to overcome stuttering, too. Since then I have always had a real compassion for people who stutter. I have been able to help several people overcome it. Have you had any experience in helping people who stutter?"

What a surprise! I was so taken aback, I think I must have stuttered a little on my own! I immediately recovered, and we had an engrossing conversation for the next hour on some of the issues involved in stuttering. I knew this man for another fifteen years before his death. From then on I continued to wonder how on earth he could publish some of the stuff he did, but I felt treated as a person by him. I was always at home with him. I learned to have a quiet heart in relation to him, free of disgust. He silenced my noisy heart by his capacity for empathy and self-revelation. He taught me to do that in relation to others who have preconceived notions about me. Serenity becomes more distinctly yours as class-action thinking ceases to create noise in your heart.

In the second place, when you examine closely the prejudice that causes you to treat other persons as common and unclean, you discover the speck that you see in their eye is a plank in your own. Whereas my friend was saying words in his magazine that I would not use, he was saying them in a rigid, perfectionistic, demanding way that was me. I was just as intolerant of him as he seemed to be of other people. He was one of the most intolerant people I had ever tolerated. He, nevertheless, was no more intolerant of others than I was intolerant of him. My disgust with him was my own intolerant, perfectionistic, demanding self which I saw in him. I was not only being tempted; I was succumbing to the thing in myself that I was condemning in him. Yet, there was more to him than just his magazine. He had the capacity to identify with an intolerant person like me. He reminded me of Edwin Markham's poem:

> He drew a circle that shut me out—
> Rebel, heretic, a thing to flout.
> But Love and I had a wit to win:
> We drew a circle that took him in.[2]

Take a New Look at Your Self-Loathing

A very battered and self-depreciating counselee said to me, "When I come to see you and the two medical students working with you, you point out the things that are good, strong, and beautiful in me. You never tell me what is wrong with me. Why?"

I replied, "Well, I will tell you what is wrong with you. You yourself are always pointing out what is wrong with you. We do not have to do that. You are doing it full time yourself. We do have other people who come to us who never seem to have a harsh word to say about themselves, and we are very different with them from the way we are with you."

Her better self had become a stranger within her. She had trouble recognizing anything good in herself. Is this true of you? Maybe you say only the very, very best things about other people. All the while you despise yourself. How can this noise be silenced long enough for the acceptable, worthy, and creative you to have a chance to become known, to be less of a stranger?

First, remember that you are not the first person to think this way about yourself. The psalmist did also:

> You have caused my companions to shun me;
> > you have made me a thing of horror to them.
> I am shut in so that I cannot escape;
> > my eye grows dim through sorrow. [Psalm 88:8-9]

Jeremiah regretted:

> Cursed be the day
>   on which I was born!
> The day when my mother bore me
>   let it not be blessed! [Jeremiah 20:14]

You are not alone. Neither are you right. You are a person of worth especially to be treasured in what is best called self-respect. You have placed the low-rated price tag on yourself. Your sense of worthlessness is a roaring complaint in your heart. As the Psalmist again says, "I think of God, and I moan; I meditate, and my spirit faints" (Psalm 77:3).

In the second place, check your self-appraisal with that of someone else. You may believe you are thinking too highly of yourself. You keep telling yourself how valuable you really are, but all sorts of strange echoes are in your heart. Even good news about yourself you can turn around and hear as bad news! So, let other people be a testing influence for you. They just may become the bearers of good news to you in the face of all the bad news you have been giving yourself. I find myself constantly taking off the low price tags from people that they themselves have put there. I try to replace them with a more factual appraisal. The process of introducing them to their value as persons hopefully increases their capacity to hear the friendly image of God into which they are made. They have trouble believing that even God can love them. You may have that trouble too.

I recall such a person who told me that he believed God could love all humanity, but the man had great trouble believing God could love such a worthless person as he felt himself to be. He said, "I am in the position of the man in the Bible who said, 'I believe; help my unbelief'" The most fertile source of a noisy heart is disbelief of good news: the unwillingness of persons, maybe like yourself, to accept, meet, and get acquainted with the stranger within them that is valuable, worthy, loved and gifted by God.

The nearer you get to that worthy self, the more you let the strange noises become welcome residents in your heart's awareness.

You sense more security and peace. A quietness comes over you. Furthermore, your exiled, worthful self is ultimately the Christ in you, the restored image of God within you. It is little wonder, is it, that you can hear the worst sounds in your heart more easily than you can the music of the best sound in you? You consider yourself a foreigner to this central Eternal One within you. However, the more you journey into your deepest self, the more you get acquainted with God, whose spirit is in you. Little wonder Robert Browning has David say to Saul:

> O Saul, it shall be
> A Face like my face that receives thee; a Man like to me,
> Thou shalt love and be loved, forever: a Hand like
>   this hand
> Shall throw open the gates of a new life to thee!
>   See the Christ
> Stand![3]

chapter five

SILENCES

YOU CANNOT

SAFELY IGNORE

I know very little about flying a plane. However, as a passenger, I have listened to the noises of planes enough to know which noises indicate that the plane is working right. Not long before a destination is reached, the engines are throttled down and become quieter. Just before the final approach for landing, I hear the gear being let down and locking into place with a reassuring "clunk."

I don't think the pilots nor any experienced passengers could afford to ignore engine noises that did not become quieter or landing gear that did not go "clunk" at the appropriate time. Such missing noise, or silence, is a sign of real trouble.

Life is like that. Some very important silences are indications that serious trouble is approaching, very near, or right upon you. You cannot afford to ignore these silences. You can ignore them; many people do so; no one does so safely. These silences are prophetic silences: they are filled with messages from God about critical conditions in your present, unlearned lessons from your past, and the shape of things to come for your future. In my work as a pastoral counselor, I saw enough after-the-fact tragedy to ask, "Why didn't someone notice what was going wrong earlier? Why did they ignore the troubled silences that preceded this tragedy?" Ignoring these deadly silences can be followed by events that leave permanent noises in your heart—regrets. You build in misgivings, distresses of heart, and qualms of conscience that continue to rumble around in your heart. Consequently, one way to nurture a healing silence in a noisy heart is to retune your antennae for these silences you cannot afford to ignore. The "rackets" in your heart may well be prevented now by listening closely to the silences. I shall describe a few.

The Silence of a Seemingly Happy Child

The first silence you cannot afford to ignore is that of a child who, over a long period of time, ceases to protest being separated from you. You may place this child of yours in the hands of one round-the-clock babysitter after another while you are busy. You may justify doing so in a hundred ways. The child can understand and accept only one: the hard reality that you are forced to do so against your will in order to provide the absolute necessities of life—food, shelter, and clothing. If your explanations are dishonest, trivial, or selfish, the child will tend to sense it without your saying so. Even if you do not appreciate no-word communication, your child is expert at it.

You may leave your child and be very bothered that he or she protests loudly. Then, one day, the protests silence. The child seems sad for a while. Then you note that he or she becomes interested in toys, food, and maybe a pet.

Of one such child a mother said, "[He] ruined everything for me. He ended my career. He threatened my marriage. Now I ask myself what have I done that caused this problem between us."[1]

Yet the child was detached from his mother, and of himself he replied to this therapist, "Every sound is different. And there are some sounds I don't make, but they happen. Thunder is a sound. And dropping things makes sounds. And I can be so quiet. I can make no noise at all. I can make silence."[2]

His mother, a remarkable woman, did notice his silence to the point that she became concerned. She heard his silence, and thought he was retarded or schizophrenic. She found the help they both needed. Finally, when she found herself proud of him, grateful for him, and attached to him, she found a warm, loving child with superior ability.

The peaceful, undemanding, silent child can well be the child who has given up and gotten past hurting about his or her need for reliable, intimate parenting. When he or she gives up, the cries of protest cease. The child discovers he or she can "make silence." As John Bowlby, the English psychiatrist says, "After a series of upsets at losing mother figures," a child will "act as if neither mothering nor contact with humans has much significance for him."[3] The lapse into silence can be deafening to all but the deaf. The "good child" is not necessarily at peace or happy.

The Silence of a Desperate Marriage Partner

Have you ever listened to a man or a woman whose marriage partner has just announced the intention of getting a divorce? Or, perhaps, instead of announcing it, the mate simply walked into the house, packed his or her things, and moved out without prior notice of any kind? The abandoned partner says, "I didn't have the slightest idea anything was wrong. Things have been just like they always were. Now—with no warning, like a bolt out of the blue—she tells me our marriage is dead. What on earth has gotten into him?"

Your friend or relative is in shock. Or it may have been you. No reasoning gets through and, whether you are a man or a woman, in such shock you are likely to become hysterical with fear of the unknown. This trauma has broken the thin coverings of life. You are exposed to the raw elements. It looks bleak. You feel numb, cold, bereft.

However, if you hear both sides of the story, the spouse who does the leaving is likely to say, "I have been trying to get through to him for years to no avail. He buries his head in the sand. Nothing I have said or done is ever heard, much less needed. Finally, about a year ago, I quit trying to get through. I just went about the chores and routines of the day, week, and month. I said no more. I have stood that as long as I can. That's no way to live."

You will note the explanation, "I said no more." That is the silence the other partner did not hear. None of us can afford to ignore silences like that.

If your partner has talked, griped, and complained, you may have gotten used to the noise. You may have said to yourself, "Oh, she is just nagging. She is just talking. If it's not one thing it's another. She has to complain about something. I just let it go in one ear and out the other. It does not bother me. That's just the way she is. Nothing is going to stop it."

Then the partner who has been talking, complaining, nagging, ceases to do so. She covers over the sudden silence very well. She takes on extra work or simply isn't there any more. If you are the mate, you simply enjoy the silence, the peace and quiet. You can have more time for doing things with your friends. Or, he may sign up for travel duty on the job or change jobs to one that calls for him to be away from home most of the time. Or, she intensifies the effort, now working night and day. If the wife ceases to complain and nag she may cover the silence by becoming interested in going back to school—full time—over and above an already overloaded schedule. She may be a woman who has a salaried position or works in one of the professions. She takes on more and more duties, working nights and weekends. The noise has ceased, only because distance has put it out of earshot, though a reasonably sensitive ear of the heart can hear.

When the issues on which you have given up trying to talk about take the soundless form of behavior, you can suffer in silences of this sort for months or years, until finally one of you decides to move out and live alone, to stop pretending. The other then says, "What on earth has happened? I thought you were perfectly happy. I was." One of you failed to notice the silence, which may have begun weeks, months, even years ago.

Marriages are filled with song, laughter, teasing, touching, and conversation. Both partners participate evenly. When these noises cease, deafness to the silences in marriage can be attributed to several faulty assumptions. You cannot safely assume that marriage as an institution will automatically ensure the health of your relationship. If you do so, you fail to take your mate seriously. You become a superficial person yourself. You hazard the basic well-being of your marriage. Also, you may falsely assume that your marriage will not change, decay, or die if you do not both nourish attentiveness to what each other is saying. Even the best marriage is very fragile; it takes constant attention. Love is made up of attention, considerateness, and care. Silence—in the negative sense—is that which you have chosen not to pay attention to, to fail to pay attention. You selectively ignore what your mate is saying. Silence is that which you do not consider important enough to respond to. In a marriage this is the silence you cannot safely ignore—unless you want to kill your marriage.

The Silence of a Rejected Parent

Some glossy magazines and pop psychology books would have you conclude that only sons and daughters suffer rejection. They wrongly cause you to blame yourself for all your son's or daughter's dilemmas. This is a half-truth that often prompts parents to give all they have to therapist after therapist, seeking to put their son or daughter back together again. Yet the other half of the truth is equally important: the son or daughter—even as young as two or three—has a mind of his or her own. Certainly, school-age children make decisions, feel a sense of power, and know how to control many situations. But children of most age levels can use words, actions, and silence to protest, to reject the words, actions, and silence of their parents.

Parents have feelings too. Parents feel rejected too. Parents can be hurt too. Parents, one might go so far as to say, are people too. As Paul Adams, a child psychiatrist, says, "When we are evaluating parents as parents, we need . . . to get glimpses of them as persons with inner lives that sometimes overflow the more public, conventionalized images that they present to us."[4] If this is an important thing for a psychotherapist to do, how much more important it is for you to feel and do in relation to your own parents.

Do your parents tend to lecture you, to exhort you, impress things upon you, try to control you? Yes! Yes! And you continually protest? Then watch out for the day your parents cease doing all these things. At first they—or one of them—become somewhat sad, distant, and depressed. You hear your parent sigh deeply and say, "Well, I've got to go to work." Or, the parent ceases to be as fussy, as solicitous, or as talkative. A superficial warmth and smile takes the place of all this. The parent is kind and decent, but distant and certainly inexpressive of his or her feelings. All the old furor, fuming, fretting roaring, and complaining are gone. It is like visiting a battlefield at Verdun or Normandy Beach. All is still and quiet.

Your parent may have less education than you do. When you passed what he or she knows, you began to put distance between you. Conflict roared for a while. Then silence ensued. Your parent either gave up or withdrew—or both. Or perhaps you may have the same amount of education as your parent. Yet you put him or her down, disparaged and lorded it over him or her, until finally he or she just hushed.

Or, you may have had much better luck financially than your father and mother. You live in a better house than they do. You send your children to a prestigious private school rather than to a public school such as you attended. You wear better clothes than they do. You may have taken up habits of drinking and heavy socializing. You have forgotten or are trying to forget some of the values they gave you. You may have joined a more sophisticated church than that to which your parents belong.

At first, they put up great resistance to all these changes. Then they gave up, withdrew, quit coming to see you, calling you, or mingling with your friends. You, on the other hand, may feel that your parents are backward, and uncouth. You are uneasy with them, have little time for them, and do only your "duty" in relation to them.

But listen to their silence.

In all these instances, your parent or parents feel the sting of your rejection. Parents react the same way other people do when rejected. They become hostile at first, even combative with words or fists. Then they become despairing. Finally, they give up and mourn in silence. Do you hear their silence? These are silences you cannot afford to ignore.

Paying attention to these silences and breaking through to your parents offer you a ready source for nurturing the qualmy noises in your own heart. You have the opportunity to reintroduce yourself to your parents as another adult who just also happens to be their son or daughter. You can explore with them some of the human strengths they have conferred upon you. You can tell them that you are aware of and bothered by the worlds of pain the years have brought each of you. You can be comrades with them and not just a child of them. Isn't movement from parent to child to adult to a mature comradeship long overdue? You have no guarantee or control as to whether they will be able to respond as I have suggested they might. They may not even want to do so. Yet, you will know that you honestly tried.

Furthermore, you can search with your parents for new things that they are interested in from which you can learn. Maybe they have taken up square dancing, reading books that you never thought they would, or lobbying on political issues you never expected. What on earth have they been up to, anyhow? Not only can you have a private life; so can they, now that you are not watching.

More than that, they are authorities on you. They probably have kept track of you when you thought they had forgotten. They are authorities, too, on pain. They probably have suffered more illnesses than you have, although not necessarily so. They can introduce both you and your children—if you have children—to the real part that death is of life. They are your own children's roots. They can inform and advise your children of their and your heritage.

Otherwise, a benevolent conspiracy (and sometimes not so benevolent) can grow up between your own children and your parents. Someone has said the reason grandparents and grandchildren often get along so well is that they have a common enemy! Need this be so? I think not. Avoid it by hearing and heeding the sound of your parents' silence.

The Unheard Silence of Another Person's Decision to Die

An uncanny silence that you cannot afford to ignore is the decision of someone close to you that life is over. It is not uncommon for a person to decide that life is ending through disease or length of years or both. Another may decide to end life in suicide. The aged, the terminally ill, and the suicidal ones at some time or other cut off communication—unless those around them are supersensitive to silence.

You may have a relative or friend who is quite old. A few years ago the person's complaint was, "I am being shoved aside because of my age." A few months ago the complaint was, "I have been laid on the shelf." Months pass and you hear nothing from your friend. Every so often you think, "I wonder how he is getting along. I haven't heard from him in a long time." You plan to visit or to telephone. But you procrastinate. Then you renew your resolve and obey the impulse. You find a wan, listless person, difficult to converse with. His enthusiasm then "kicks on," conversation becomes easy, and laughter is heard. You leave or hang up the phone, and you feel that listening to the sounds of his silence paid off, not only for him but for you. You were able to express appreciation for what that person had meant to you over the years. Gratitude expressed is a good feeling.

You have also faced the fact of aging in yourself. You are as much older than the last time you saw her as she is. You will need someone to mean to you what you have tried to mean to her. Practically speaking, you will do well to have friends younger than yourself who will remember you later.

A fifteen-year-old girl was sent by her parents to converse with me about her life situation. She asked, "Why would you take up time talking with a person my age?"

I explained, "I am sixty. You are fifteen. When I am ninety, Liz you will be forty-five. You see, you are four times younger than I am now. Then you will only be twice as young. I will, nevertheless, be quite old. Then I will need someone like you to remember me and come to see me again! I need you as my friend."

Another person you notice a silence from is the depressed or suicidal person. You have a relative or friend who has usually called you by telephone, come to see you, done projects together with you. You notice a blackout of communication and initiative. If it persists, your first question is, "I wonder if she is angry at me? What's happened?" You might learn to ask, "I wonder if she is discouraged or depressed?" The chances are that you have done nothing to make her angry. Yet if you take the initiative and move toward her, you will find a sad, morose person. The stimulus of your visit may make the difference between hope and despair.

Suicidal persons may talk about their intention to kill themselves in spite of the common false assumption that people who talk about suicide never do so. It is when that person ceases to talk about suicide that he is more likely to do so. The person may say, even upon close questioning, "Everything is beautiful. I am getting along better than ever before in my life." You should ask, "What happened to make such a sudden improvement." This silence is one that calls for a double alert that you might extend by telling the person's family physician, minister, and close family members. However, you may hesitate: Is this not a confidential matter? No. It is not. Suicide and homicide threats are not confidential. They are—if put into action— widespread in their consequences. Such threats must be handled carefully and wisely, but they are not confidential.

The threat of suicide comes in a package of glossed-over silence. If this person is close to you as a relative or friend, the change in the feeling of closeness should make you vaguely uneasy. Something is going on that you cannot quite put into words. The silence perturbs you. It creates a noise in your heart. At the very least, you can stay with and be with the person as much as possible. At the most, you can see to it with all the urgency with which you would respond to a high fever, that he or she gets to a doctor. Your attention to the silence is the thing that makes you special to the person.

The Sudden Silence of a Talkative Colleague

In business, in the professions, in churches, hospitals, and schools the ongoing group life of the working organization can be gauged by the kinds of noise the working task force of colleagues makes. The counterculture language used to speak of these noises as "vibes." Different members of a group like this have varying convictions about the way to go about doing business with each other. They differ about the directions and goals of the task force as a whole. In informal discussions and formal meetings, these convictions are expressed. You probably belong to and function in such task groups. You are challenged by the work you do with the group. Your work fits in with or runs counter to the way the group is going. You negotiate, propose changes, lobby for certain programs, and seek to arbitrate opinions contrary to your own. You aim to please and knock yourself out trying to do so.

Then one day, or even a series of days, you despair of the whole operation. You are left out of difficult decisions, many of which you have to put into effect but with which you disagree. You are ignored. You are not heeded. Nothing you say or do matters. You give up. You cease trying to influence the process. You become silent. The question before the leader of the group is whether he or she can hear your silence. Or is the leader so preoccupied with the noise of solemn assembly that silences of previously articulate persons are not heard?

If you are the leader, these questions say loudly that preoccupation keeps you from hearing both what people are saying to you and the silences that happen when they quit taking and start doing things. You discover that the people who were complaining loudly quit talking to you and the other decision makers. Then they start talking by telephone, at coffee breaks, and at lunch time with other dissatisfied persons. You begin to get negative reports from such sources. You begin to feel outflanked. What they say is just true enough to make you uncomfortable, but not true enough for you to let it distract your attention from your preoccupation with your own concerns, your own image, your own ambitions—whatever they may be.

Now, a second phase takes place: You cease to hear criticisms of you from the coffee times, the corridors, and the luncheon groups. You hear nothing. You assume to your own detriment that the dissidents have given up or that the whole situation was trivial in the first place. Like a storm it blew over in a day or two. A fatal mistake! What has happened is that they have decided to take matters into their own hands.

Another possible set of responses can follow the blackout of communication, the deadly silence. The discontented members of the group can jell into a subgroup of their own. Duly authorized meetings of subgroups of a church board, for example—such as a department group or a standing committee—can meet for their official purposes. They get blown off their course by their discontent. Confusion arises. They try to bring order out of chaos. At the exhaustion level of fatigue they resort to counsels of desperation. The critical issue is: How can we connect up again with our leaders?

The leader—by not listening to a silence he or she could not afford to ignore—has unwittingly created a power vacuum. Anything can happen.

The Silence of Your Own Ideals

In your own heart you hear noises. Many of these are your hungers for companionship, your restless ambitions, and your competitive strivings. You can quiet these down. You also have private silences of heart you cannot afford to ignore. You have ideals, dreams, aspirations, and feelings of destiny that are uniquely yours. You may be accustomed to the purring of the motors of these motivations which provide a lofty view of life for you. You may feel the surge of these callings like a fever in your pulse. John Masefield did:

> I must down to the seas again, for the call of the
> running tide
> Is a wild call and a clear call that may not be denied.[5]

But, then again, can it be denied? Yes, it can. You have become accustomed to hearing the claims of your own best self, the validity of your inner convictions, and the drive of your own clear-cut commitments in life. Yet many things may have happened to shake these certainties. You may have become disillusioned, cynical, and maybe even callous. These ideals are silenced.

You have gone a long time since you were filled with a sense of awe in the presence of the best self you essentially are. As Immanuel Kant said, "Two things fill the mind with ever new and increasing admiration and awe, the oftener and more steadily we reflect upon them: *the starry heavens above and the moral law within.*"[6] Yet for you that awe is silenced. The stirring notes of that awe's *Finlandia,* or *Ninth Symphony* in your life are not heard. They are silenced. The gun of reality has silenced them.

What were these realities? Let me consult my own heart and suggest a few things that may have silenced your dreams, aspirations, and calling:

— Ideals are fine, but you, your children, and spouse can't eat them. You have got to make a living.

— You dream of a world free of war, but the enemy has guns and you do not.

— A calling is fine and much needed, but ecclesiastical politics differ from Watergate in only one respect—the Watergate folks had somebody to catch them. The ecclesiastical politicians do not.

— You were slated for promotion. You made the "mistake" of speaking your mind on the ideals of service, quality of production, and fair dealing with the consumer. You are treated cordially. You get the cost of living increases. You do not get the promotion nor the merit raises.

— Dreams are great; visions of possibilities in life abound; but the bureaucratic hidden curriculum rewards conformity, stifles creativity, and magnifies mediocrity in the processes of degrees, certification, accreditation, etc.

Therefore, you become like one of those whom you despise. You silence your ideals, aspirations, dreams, and calling. It hurts too badly to feel them. A still, sad music of humanity plays faintly in the background, but you have deadened your own ideals. To change the figure of speech, the chords of music with which they enlivened your step are silent. They are broken. Let's change the metaphor again. The engines of your motivation have been silenced. Thank God you are in a plane that will glide. You know how to glide. You simply glide on past accomplishments, accrued seniority, and plenty of fringe benefits and perquisites of office. All you can hear is the whish of the wind around you.

A silence that you cannot afford to ignore has put you on a new course, into a set of habits not native to you. Survival is your main objective now, not the higher needs of fulfilling your ideals.

Am I anywhere near where you are? If not, you may want to write down your own list. Why not write down what caused you to give up, to silence your best impulses, and to pawn your integrity in the process?

I would prefer that you and I be more like the pilot in Antoine de Saint Exupéry's *Wind, Sand and Stars* on his way to his plane at the airport. He rides with a busload of worn-out clerks who talked of illness, money, domestic cares, and trivia. He observes them and reflects within himself:

> Old bureaucrat, my comrade, it is not you who are to blame. No one ever helped you to escape. You, like a termite, built your peace by blocking up with cement every chink and cranny through which the light might pierce. You rolled yourself up into a ball in your genteel security, in routine, in the stifling conventions of provincial life, raising a modest rampart against the winds and the tides and the stars. You have chosen not to be perturbed by great problems, having trouble enough to forget your own fate as man. You are not the dweller upon an errant planet and do not ask yourself questions to which there are no answers. You are a petty bourgeois of Toulouse. Nobody grasped you by the shoulder while there was still time. Now the clay of which you were shaped has dried and hardened, and naught in you will ever awaken the sleeping musician, the poet, the astronomer that possibly inhabited you in the beginning.
>
> The squall has ceased to be the cause of my complaint. The magic of the craft has opened for me a world in which I shall confront, within two hours, the black dragons and the crowned crests of a comb of blue lightnings, and when night has fallen, I, delivered, shall read my course in the stars.[7]

What can you do about your silenced ideals? How can you start once again being "perturbed by great problems"? How can you once again have the courage to ask questions to which there are no answers? I am a fairly weather-beaten veteran at being tempted to "shush" my own ideals. I have asked myself, "If you have given in to the temptation, and you have, how did you restore—or have restored for you—the voice of your own ideals?"

Take a look at cynicism as the silencer. Cynicism, our younger son tells me, comes from having functioned at top efficiency but without being rewarded or appreciated. The disparity between your commitment and the feedback of appreciation is too great. You become disheartened. You cut out, give up, and become a cynical, snapping, grumping faultfinder who denies the goodness of human motives or any hope for human nature. From a series of encounters with people who have deceived you, you conclude that all persons are liars. You turn the year of the Dog Star, *Kyon* in Greek, after which cynics are named, into a way of life. One year stamps you for life. You cease to trust all people. You cease to commit yourself to anyone. You throw everything you have into a job, a project, a cause. What do you get? Another day older and deeper in debt. Therefore you keep your ideals but you cease to let them guide your behavior. They are for your private museum of ideals. You shut yourself within yourself and let the liars have at it. Are you this cynical?

Or have you tried instead forming new relationships with other people who do appreciate your efforts and reward them? If you do this instead of fretting year after year, then the chords of your ideals will vibrate once more. Instead of a deafening silence of hope and aspiration, you will have music, even though your past experience will make you a more expert listener!

Now, take a look at the way you have bought into the appraisals others have made of you. They may have resisted, rejected, cheated, and said all manner of evil against you. The critical issue is whether you take their appraisal at face value and agree with their deprecia- tion of you. If you have done that, no wonder your previous ideals no longer speak up to the contrary. They have been effectively silenced by your own agreement with those who reject you. If you bought into these negative appraisals, you can sell out of them also. Start by asking for the estimate of a few nonbiased people. Get more than one. I think you need outside consultation. I get such consultation regularly myself. One such person to whom I went was my graduate-school supervising professor, Gaines S. Dobbins. I often told him that he believed in me when I did not believe in myself. Such persons can be as if God were speaking to you through them.

The next important step is to lay out the whole estimate of yourself before God in your inner thoughts. And this presents another silence you cannot afford to ignore.

The Silence of God and the Futility of Prayer

You may have already noticed that your communication with God is silent, too. You may be like Job:

> My days are past, my plans are broken off,
>   the desires of my heart. [Job 17:11]

> God has put me in the wrong,
>   and closed his net around me.
> Even when I cry out, "Violence!" I am not answered;
>   I call aloud, but there is no justice. [Job 19:6-7]

The silence of God is a dreadful silence that you cannot afford to ignore. Your questioning of God's silence puts you in good company with Job again. Your feeling of "no reward" may be like his:

> What is the Almighty, that we should serve him?
>   And what profit do we get if we pray to him?
> [Job 21:15]

If you feel this way, I am in the same jam as were Job's counselors:

> How then will you comfort me with empty nothmgs?
>   There is nothing left of your answers but falsehood.
> [Job 21:34]

You bring a maze of conflicting feelings to your consultation with God similar to Job's. God knows this. You are alone before God. You frankly confess that, as Francis Thompson says, "human love needs human meriting."[8] Yet you plunge deeper into your inner being and agree with Thompson again:

> There is no expeditious road
> To pack and label men for God,
> And save them by the barrel-load.[9]

Then, you discover afresh the Center of you that is not you—it is God. You begin to realize what has happened.

You have pursued your idealism, your aspirations, your hopes until they turned to ashes. Yet in the pursuit of them you have been running from God without at all intending to do so—all the while thinking you were headed straight toward God. The nautical error of calculation had you fixed on the graceless search for a graceless merit—human merit. You valued your goals, aspirations, and hopes in terms of winning and in the process caused someone else to lose. This may be what you mean by "appreciation" or "merit." All human love needs human meriting. Yet you have met with a Love that is more than human love. Your merit in God's assessment of you is the value you have because you are related to, treasured by, and made for companionship with God. God then gives you a gentle response: "All things fly thee, for thou fliest me."[10]

A rabbi was being threatened for his life by a gang of mobsters. They wanted his property. He would not capitulate. His wife asked him to arm himself and fight fire with fire. He refused. She—in her desperation—felt that he was a coward, and said so. That hurt. He thought for a long time before he said, "I fear two things—that I would do something displeasing to God, and that I would lose your, my wife's, respect."

Fear causes you to get out of earshot of your own personal integrity. The North Star for correcting your course is the love of God and neighbor, in that order. To get them reversed—to rely upon the love of neighbor first and then upon God—is to make a 180-degree reversal from the relationship that sooner or later produces the silence of God. All things and purposes—apart from the search first for the kingdom of God—flee us. To search for these first is a flight from reality. You do not have to seek the approval of everyone around you in order to be a person in your own right . . . any more than you have to do things out of their rejection of you that assure they will reject you. You can make a 180-degree turn and cease such a flight from God and God's love.

At the dawn of a new relationship, the hostile silence you felt at the thought of God changes from a cold, empty, threatening silence into a warm, full, and reassuring silence that simply says, "You are not alone. I am with you." Companionship with God takes the place of your hostility, a creative solitude erases your loneliness. Then you become all that you are capable of being—in a way free of self-consciousness.

chapter six

THE SERENITY

RESPONSE

TO SILENCE'S CALL

You have read thus far. Has silence waylaid you yet? Sometimes you do not have to hunt for silence. It ambushes you with joy, peace, and inner courage. At other times silence comes to you as a gift. You meet a friend whose silent care is contagious. God gives you silence in response to your own prayer for a noise-free heart. You pray, "Lord, grant me silence in the inner person, and may the outward person and the inward person be the same." Or you may pray, "Grant me the serenity to accept things that cannot be changed, the courage to change the things that can be changed, and the wisdom to know the difference."

Yet silence comes more often as the internal response of serenity to the call to silence. The practice of silence becomes a chosen way of life for you. Your response of serenity is an ethical response: You choose between the varied kinds of serenity. The silence of a noise-free heart is the result.

You choose between different kinds of serenity responses. To be serene, you place your trust in something or someone. You practice the disciplines that trusting this thing, cause, or person demands. You set your heart upon one among many kinds of serenity. Out of a list of several kinds of serenity you can decide which ones you will choose.

Serenity Response Number One: "I have it made." You may assume that when you have reached the top, you can be serene. This is a very old serenity response. Emperors were addressed as "Your Serenity." Bishops and popes were called "Your Serene Highness." The great industrial pioneers early set a Horatio Alger picture of success before Americans. They believed that anyone who just wanted to and tried hard enough could reach the top. Jesus speaks of the man who had many possessions and holdings. He said to himself, "Man, you have plenty of good things laid by, enough for many years: take life easy, eat, drink and enjoy yourself" (Luke 12:19, NEB). Such a response of serenity may be a security operation. If one has laid aside for a rainy day, life can be looked upon as free of noise in the heart. In the peak years of life, one's serenity and way of quieting the noise in one's heart is to buy something that will be conspicuous evidence of having arrived. Thus one is beyond the heart of turbulence of ordinary persons in the human lot. For some of us in some of our lives and for some of us in all of our lives, holding power over the lives of other people is the highest good and source of serenity. The "You have it made" response of serenity depends upon a distant, future goal of life. You endure all sorts of drudgery with the faith that doing so will pay off in the long future. Your serenity comes at the end you have in mind. You hope for the ease that comes. You lay up, store up, and accumulate. On a rainy day you will eat, drink, and enjoy yourself. Having it made, having arrived—is this your source of serenity? Have you set your heart upon this?

Serenity Response Number Two: "I am able to take it." This is the response of self-sufficiency, of personal competence. You may find it a mixed blessing. At one stage in your life this response is the only way through the gnawing and vexing anxiety in your heart. You were born helpless. You had to be fed, cleaned, clothed, taught to walk. Through adolescence you struggled. You had no money, and few persons were willing to give you work or let you learn. You may even have found that your own parents did not seem eager to teach you to work. You may have gotten used to this kind of dependency and concluded that your best chance for security was to get someone else to support you. Whether you are a man or woman, this is a hazardous search for serenity. Self-sufficiency cannot be deleted from life. It is one of the biological goals of life to be sought and accomplished.

However, while you are becoming competent, you may develop a habit system that makes self-sufficiency a way of life, not a transitional biological goal for the early years of your life. You can make a case for self-sufficiency in the sense of being competent. You choose not to carry into life a lifestyle of inferiority. You develop skills and competencies that give you a wider range of serenity than you would have if you did not become competent in this way. In fact, if you are a professional person, seeing other people or yourself work in an incompetent manner creates noise in your heart. It bugs you. You can overlook almost anything except sloppy, careless work. You assess people primarily by their competence. Serenity for you comes upon having finished a job and having done it well, whether it was a pleasant and enjoyable task or not. Having more than one competency gives you a feeling of freedom and serenity also. You can do more than one thing with zest, just as well. You are a resourceful person. You find serenity in your resourcefulness. You can take it.

Yet such resourcefulness can be the center of your deepest loneliness. You are made not for self-sufficiency but for communion with other persons and with God. You get an eerie, creeping noise in your heart that is more like mildew: being shut up and shut off in your own self-sufficiency. You may be one who thinks and feels as did William Ernest Henley:

> In the fell clutch of circumstance,
> I have not winced nor cried aloud:
> Under the bludgeonings of chance
> My head is bloody but unbowed.[1]

Is this "I Can Take It" stance of heart the source of your serenity, the quieting of the noise in your heart?

Serenity Response Number Three: "Life is lived best when lived in cold blood." The human being is by nature a warm-blooded animal. Yet one of the images of serenity that manages the lives of many people is that of seeing themselves as strong, silent, feelingless—able to do all things in cold blood. Many of the things you do call for a hemostat on the artery of personal feelings. If you are a pilot of a plane that carries three hundred passengers, you cannot afford to be a handwringer in a storm. If you are a surgeon, you cannot faint at the sight of blood. If you are a construction worker on a tall building, you cannot have a fear of heights. If you make your living as a public speaker, you have pushed stage fright back into the furthest corner of your heart. You do many of these and other things without feeling, somewhat in cold blood.

Yet you are not always flying a plane, performing surgery, working on a tall building. or speaking from a public platform. You may, however, have chosen to live your whole life in feelingless squelching of the noise of warm blood running through your heart, the chatter of contradictory emotions, and the shrill protests at being abandoned by someone who means a lot to you. If this is your particular style of serenity in response to the call to silence, take a new look at it. Do you communicate that you really don't care, or that you can't care?

Serenity Response Number Four: "I have gotten my life together." Think of your heart as pieces unrelated to each other. Think of your life as a group of separate tribes with no appreciation of each other and no desire to get together, constantly at odds with each other. Think of your heart as a set of competing desires, each of which demands total satisfaction while all the others scream with hunger. What a set of double screams! They are screaming in stereo. You can hardly hear yourself think.

Whichever figure of speech comes home to you best, now imagine that the pieces are fitted together into a completed picture. Imagine that the tribes have sat down together and made peace. Imagine that the competing desires have suddenly learned to respect each other, to settle for partial satisfaction, and to share with the other desire. No one desire now dominates the scene. You are getting your life together. Now these pieces, tribes, or desires become resources within you. You can draw upon them to meet the demands of the world around you without being unduly anxious, afraid, or conflict-ridden. You approach life with a serenity that is calmness, a faith in yourself, others, and God that is certainty, and a sense of peace that amounts to courage. You are not worried about having it made; you know that there are some things in life you do not have to take; and you find your deepest satisfaction is caring for other people. You have it together. This is the serenity response to the call to silence I commend to you.

The Christian response of serenity to the call of silence is a very personal getting it all together. The apostle Paul said, "I have learned to find resources in myself whatever my circumstances. I know what it is to be brought low, and I know what it is to have plenty. I have been very thoroughly initiated into the human lot with all its ups and downs—fullness and hunger, plenty and want. I have strength for anything through him [Christ] who gives me power" (Philippians 4:11-13, NEB). He had it all together, but he did not think that the source of his power was totally himself. He had found the power of an indwelling Presence of Christ within. In another place he could say, "I have been crucified with Christ: the life I now live is not my life, but the life which Christ lives in me . . ." (Galatians 2:20, NEB). His resources within himself were not lonely resources; they were shared resources with his inner comradeship with Christ. In Christ you are kept together as a human being, as a coherent friend to others, and in fellowship with Christ.

But you will say, "You have pointed out the choices I have as to my particular serenity response. By a process of elimination you have arrived at the particular serenity response you would recommend. Now, for crying out loud, can we get to it? Be practical! What are some specifics as to how I can practice silence of heart? Describe the inner workings of the practice of silence."

Some things can be said that have not already been said about the practice of silence. A rearview-mirror glance at the ground we have already covered gives a quick look at suggestions previously made about the practice of silence. I will list some of these in the form of questions that will serve both as a check list for you and a summary of suggestions already discussed. Then I can make some additional remarks about the practice of silence.

A Practice-of-Silence Test

1. What place and time are the quietest for you to experience silence in your regular day's routine?

2. Who in your life creates the most uproar, confusion, and stress? What have you done to change this? Do you prefer the uproar to silence?

3. What choices do you have to accomplish your day's work in a quieter, more stress-free way? To unload some of the sensory, overload of your day?

4. List pockets of silence in your work arena.

5. What recent use of no-word language have you noted?

6. Has your need to have the first and last words changed in any specific way, such as you making note of it even?

7. What kinds of jabbering go on in your working-group life, and what have you done to lower the noise level for yourself and others?

8. Have you experimented with listening with your other four senses—seeing, touching, tasting, smelling—as well as hearing?

9. Have you made any progress in breaking your addiction to television, telephones, radio, and stereo?

10. With your friends and family do you debrief troubles or rehash them?

11. Have you reconnected in any way with your amputated past?

12. Have you noted yourself disparaging others, or disparaging others less? Or have you not noticed it at all?

13. Have you caught yourself becoming fatigued, losing perspective, exercising poor judgment, or becoming confused? Did you immediately create some time of silence for yourself?

14. Have you taken feelings of loneliness as a challenge to seek silence, gotten away from the crowd, and exercised your right to form your private thoughts and opinions on serious matters?

15. What initiative have you taken to create specific times, places, and rituals for privacy and solitude?

16. Have you stood apart, backed off, turned aside, and broken out from your noisy overinvolvement to experience silence?

17. Do you loathe yourself less? Do you respect yourself more? Why?

18. Have you tuned yourself to listen to the silences of members of your own family?

19. At your work who used to talk a lot and does not have anything to say now? What happened to make the change?

20. Have any of your friends simply not been heard from for no apparent reason in a short while?

21. Have you lost touch with your own ideals and faced up to your cynicism?

22. Are you aware of the silent Presence of God in any personal way at all?

The practice of silence can be taken further. Specific exercises will enable you to enjoy, nurture, and savor the gifts of silence that are yours for the asking. You can have them at no cost except paying attention.

Catch Step with the Wisdom of Your Body

Richard Cabot, long-time medical director of the Massachusetts General Hospital in Boston, used to say in talking with students,

"The body has more sense than the mind." The body indeed is fearfully and wonderfully made. The thoughts behind its creation are high. We reach to attain unto these thoughts of the Creator. Paying attention to the simplest functions of your body envelops you in a world of silence. You may feel like you are scuba diving in the depths of your own being.

Pay Attention to Your Breathing. God breathed into you the breath of life and you became a living being. The gift of breathing goes unnoticed, unappreciated, unattended. Attend to it. Visualize a mental picture of the remarkable pathway your breathing of air in and out takes. Visualize the nostrils, the little eustachian tubes that connect your ears to your nasal tract. Hold your nose and very gently blow air into those tubes. Now breathe deeply into your lungs. Imagine the shape of your lungs, the internal structures that handle the air. They take in oxygen and cast off carbon dioxide. You feed plants around you with carbon dioxide as necessary for their survival as their oxygen is for you. Notice that when you are anxious and your heart fills with the noise of strife and discord, your breathing notices it too. You are breathing shorter and tighter and are getting less oxygen. When you deliberately breathe deeply, you relax and your brain gets more oxygen. You are quieter within.

Pay Attention to Your Muscles—Both Sets of Them. One of the noises in your heart may be your concern over the meaning of various pains you feel in your body. Of course, pain is an indicator that you may need to see your physician. He who has himself for a doctor has an unwise patient. Your doctor may say that there is nothing wrong with you. You may assume from this that the pain is all in your head. Your doctor means that you do not have an infection, a pulled ligament, a growth, or an infection. Yet you can have pain without having any of these. This pain may be caused by muscles that are too loose, tense, or spasming. An effective program of physical exercises prescribed by a specialist in physical medicine can teach you to pay precise attention to your muscles. You can quiet the pain by personal discipline in toning your muscles.

You have two sets of muscles—voluntary ones and involuntary ones. The involuntary ones do not pay much attention to you. You can control them indirectly by learning to practice relaxation, to search after a more serene way of life, and to let the things that are trivial go unattended. You can affect these muscles by deep-breathing exercises such as I have mentioned. You relax these areas of your body most by focusing attention upon them and thinking about relaxation. How do you do that?

Pay Attention to the Retinas of Your Closed Eyes. Many of us live in a black-and-white world. You may be such a person. You miss the wonderful world of color. One way of relaxation is to focus your attention on colors. Close your eyes. You have in each of them an instant photography laboratory. Black and white and colors can be processed instantly without cost to you. Of course, you pay attention. That is the only price. You can afford that. Now that you have closed your eyes, open them and stare hard with focused eyes at a colored wall, boot, picture, or other object. Close your eyes again and watch the colors in your retina change. Red becomes bluish; blue turns yellow; green turns yellowish; yellow turns blue-green. The big difference is that the color to which a given color turns is ten times more beautiful

In the silence of your own eyes you can see colors such as only sunsets and leaves changing colors in the fall can produce. Notice as you do so that the tense muscles in your body begin to relax. You begin to breathe more deeply. You discover the silence of your bodily processes. The great Hand that created this silence loosens and relaxes spasmed, pain-producing muscles. They say nothing. They simply let go.

Take a New Look at Your Sleepless Times. In the middle of the night, early in the morning, or just as you have gone to bed you cannot fall to sleep, get back to sleep, or stay asleep. You are restless. Your noisy heart keeps saying, "You've got to get some sleep. You've got to work tomorrow. You will be dead on your feet." You try harder. You cannot sleep. What on earth are you going to do? Quit fighting it. That's what you are going to do. You have been given a time of silence that is overdue. Take advantage of it. Please do not get up and turn the radio on or watch the late, late, late show on TV. Simply lie still and rest. Quit demanding sleep of yourself and settle for rest.

You may be struggling with a big, middle-sized, or small decision that has to be made. What is it? Define it. Do you have enough facts to decide now? If so, decide what you are going to do. If not, decide how you are going to get the facts. Lay the decision to rest. You will rest better.

Not all your memories are bad. Call up the most pleasant memories you can retrieve from that wonderful computer of your mind. Enjoy the pleasures of those memories. Think of these memories again the next time you are prone to say or do something that will remain as a vicious memory. You do not want things like that in your memory. Your memory is one of the major tributaries in your noisy heart. May it run quietly and provide rest, beauty, and pleasure for you. There are rivers that make your heart glad. The flow of memory is one of them.

Not all dreams are frightening. Even dreams of persons who have died and for whom we have grieved can be pleasant retreats from the harsh reality of their death. Do not deny yourself the happiness of the pleasant dreams you have about the deceased. Your dreams may be teaching you to talk to your friends of the good times, the laughter, and even some of the negative feelings you have about the departed loved one. Finding such a friend who will listen is not as easy as you would like it to be. They are there though. Keep looking for them. At least, you can enjoy these thoughts as you lie awake at night. Not all dreams are bad. Many of them are oases in the desert of a noisy world. Enjoy them. Drink them to the full. Doing so will help you rest.

I recall such a dream that means much to me. My grandmother was another mother for me while mine worked long hours in the mills. She taught me many things, not the least of which was to read, to love words, to pronounce and spell them correctly. She was a person who gave me unconditional love and acceptance. She died when I was twenty years old. We had little or no money. Mother did see to it that she was buried, but it took a long time to pay off the funeral expenses. The funeral was very simple. We had no food for relatives who came. Neither they nor the neighbors had food to bring. My brother put himself in debt. It pains me that I never thanked him.

Over three decades later I dreamed that my grandmother was dead and that I had the money to provide a $15,000 funeral for her. I provided a joyous, abundant wake of food and drink for everyone who would come to celebrate her life! The miracle of the dream was that she was both dead and alive. She was the person whose funeral was being held; she was also present at the funeral enjoying the party! I awakened from this dream with a warm sense of well-being. Now, as I recount this dream, I give thanks for her and for the dream. In reality, I can't get into the scene of a $15,000 funeral, but I can enjoy a dream that pushes reality aside and lets me tell my grandmother and my own self that I love her in unmistakable pictures.

Reassess Your Stance toward God

Your and my stance toward God changes from one era of our life to another. I did not become an institutionally related Christian until I was nineteen years old. I was not brought up in a particularly religious home, although my sister was an active example for me in this respect. We were simply not a churchgoing people. Yet my mother and my grandmother were God-wondering persons. God was so down-to-earth to us that we did not talk much about God. As I trace the movement of my stance toward God from one era of life to another, I see it moving from relating to the Divine as a void, to relating to God as an enemy, to relating to the Eternal One as a friend. You may find this helpful in reassessing your stance toward God. If God is felt to be a void, then emptiness, hollowness, vagueness, and an aching aloneness produce echoes in your noisy heart. If God is sensed as an enemy, then complaining, contending, refining, objecting, and even sneering roar around in your heart. If God is experienced as a friend, then resonance, sympathetic understanding, companionship, and a feeling of never being bereft sustain and soothe the sounds of silence in your heart.

Wherever you are on your pilgrimage in your relation to God, know one thing: I am a fellow pilgrim with you. You have walked with me through the pages of this book in our mutual concern to nurture silence in our noisy hearts. I would ask that the gift of courage be yours. Courage is, in essence, the faith to keep moving from the experience of God as a void or an enemy to knowing God as a steadfast Friend. In turn, you become a friend whose serenity response is to get life all together around your primary comradeship with God as a Friend. Such courage is indeed the stuff of the life of faith of which William Cowper wrote in his hymn *O for a Closer Walk with God:*

> The dearest idol I have known,
> Whate'er that idol be,
> Help me to tear it from Thy throne,
> And worship only Thee.
>
> So shall my walk be close with God,
> Calm and serene my frame;
> So purer light shall mark the road
> That leads me to the Lamb.

.

QUESTIONS FOR REFLECTION AND DISCUSSION

Chapter One
Silence for Survival and Hope

1. What does author Wayne Oates mean by "silence"? How does this compare with your understanding of silence?

2. What are the chief obstacles to silence in your life?

3. What are three ways the author looks for silence in the midst of a noisy life?

4. What might be some benefits of greater silence in your life?

5. What is the role of discernment in the nurturing of silence?

6. What does the author mean by a "noisy heart"?

7. How would you answer the "between folks" questions on pages 11 and 12? Did you derive any helpful insights from these questions?

8. What is the relationship between silence and your knowledge of God?

Chapter Two
Discovering Your Privacy in Order to Nurture Silence

1. What are some signs of the need for privacy? To what extent are you experiencing these signs?

2. How can you gain and maintain privacy without being lonely?

3. How did Jesus express his freedom from the crowd? In what ways do you need freedom from the crowd?

4. Do you feel you now have the right to private thought and judgment? How are you offering this freedom to others?

5. What places or situations in life make silence a reality for you?

6. As you look at your daily or weekly schedule, how can you create some places and times for privacy and silence?

7. Oates speaks of "quiet motions of the spirit that nurture silence." Which of these have you practiced? Which do you practice now?

Chapter Three
Down-to-Earth Centering in Silence

1. What does the author mean by "down-to-earth centering"?

2. How do you go about "centering down" your whole being or deliberately choosing a path of silence in the work of the day?

3. Have you ever experienced "a willingness to let someone else have the last word"? What happened? Is there a situation now in which you might make that choice?

4. Are there ways you could listen more with all of your senses in order to experience wordless messages?

5. How might you better deal with the telephone, television, and computer to experience more silence?

Chapter Four
Silencing the Strange Noises Within Your Heart

1. Wayne Oates speaks of the strange noises of the heart that need silencing. Which of these make noises in your heart? What can you do about them?

2. According to Oates, what can you do about the strange noises from your past? Do you need to take any of these actions?

3. Are there ways in which you experience self-loathing? What does Oates recommend as ways to deal with a low self-image?

4. What idea in this chapter was most helpful to you?

Chapter Five
Silences You Cannot Safely Ignore

1. Are there any silences in your own life that you cannot safely ignore? If you can identify some, what might you do to help the situation?

2. Are there ideals you once had that have been silenced? Do you want to revive or renew any of them? How might that be done?

3. Have you ever experienced the silence of God? Is that part of your experience now? What can you learn from Wayne Oates about how to deal with that silence?

Chapter Six
The Serenity Response to Silence's Call

1. Which of the "serenity responses" described in this chapter speak most closely to your way of life?

2. Can you add any other serenity responses?

3. The Practice-of-Silence Test summarizes many of the learnings of this book. As you answer the questions, what are the most valuable insights for you?

4. Which of the suggestions in the "Catch Step with the Wisdom of Your Body" section did you find most helpful?

5. How would you describe your current stance toward God?

NOTES

Chapter One
Silence for Survival and Hope

1. Meyer Friedman, M.D., and R.H. Rosenmann, M.D., *Type A Behavior and Your Heart* (Greenwich, CT: Fawcett Publications, 1974), pp. 246-47.

2. Blaise Pascal, *Pensées*, translated by W. F. Trotter (New York: Random House, Modern Library, 1941), par. 206, p. 74.

3. John Keats, "I Stood Tiptoe upon a Little Hill".

4. George Gordon, Lord Byron, *Childe Harold's Pilgrimage*, canto 4, "The Ocean," stanza 178.

5. Rachel Carson, *Silent Spring* (Boston: Houghton Mifflin Co., 1962), p.3.

6. Thomas Merton, "In Silence," from *The Strange Islands* (New York: New Directions, 1957), pp. 87-88.

7. Thomas Merton, *Conjectures of a Guilty Bystander* (Garden City, NY: Doubleday & Company, Inc., 1968), p. 15.

8. Hellen Keller, *The Story of My Life* (New York: Grossett and Dunlap, 1902), p. 131.

9. Søren Kierkegaard, *Purity of Heart*, in *The Doubleday Devotional Classics*, vol. 3 (Garden City, NY: Doubleday-Galilee Books, 1978), p. 127.

Chapter Two
Discovering Your Privacy in Order to Nurture Silence

1. Thomas Wolfe, "The Anatomy of Loneliness," *The American Mercury*, Oct. 1941; quoted in *Great Quotations*, compiled by George Seldes (Secaucus, NJ: Castle Books, 1966), p. 755.

2. Gustave LeBon, *The Crowd: A Study of the Popular Mind* (New York: Macmillan, 1896), pp. 29-30.

3. John Schwab, M.D., et al, "Crowding and Mental Health" (unpublished paper, Departments of Psychiatry and Sociology of the University of Florida, Gainesville, FL).

4. Robert Bolt, *A Man for All Seasons* (New York: Random House, 1962), p. xii.

5. Ibid., pp. 98 and 95

6. Dag Hammarskjöld, *Markings* (New York: Alfred A. Knopf, 1964), p. 16.

7. Elizabeth Barrett Browning, *Aurora Leigh*, Book 7.

8. Morton Kelsey, *The Other Side of Silence* (New York: Paulist Press, 1976), p. 103.

Chapter Three
Down-to-Earth Centering in Silence

1. Thomas Merton, *The Silent Life* (New York: Farrar, Strauss, and Cudahy, 1957), p. 29.

2. Thomas Merton, *Conjectures of a Guilty Bystander* (Garden City, NY: Doubleday & Company, Inc., 1968), p. 158

3. Robert Frost, "The Road Not Taken."

4. *The Journal of John Woolman*, the John Greenleaf Whittier text, in *The Doubleday Devotional Classics*, vol. II (Garden City, NY: Doubleday-Galilee Books, 1978), p. 304.

5. Alfred Korzybski, *Science and Sanity*, 3rd ed. (Lakeville, CT: Institute of General Semantics, 1948), p. 417.

6. Quoted in Jacques Hadamard, *The Psychology of Invention in the Mathematical Field* (Princeton: Princeton University Press, 1949), p. 118.

7. Ruth Deich and Patricia Hodges, *Language Without Speech* (New York: Bruner/Mazel, 1978), p. 16.

8. Miguel Unamuno, *The Tragic Sense of Life* (New York: Dover Publications, 1954), p. 196.

9. Walt Whitman, "Song of Myself", sec, 48, *Leaves of Grass*.

10. John Greenleaf Whittier, *Dear Lord and Father of Mankind.*

Chapter Four
Silencing the Strange Noises Within Your Heart

1. Johann Wolfgang von Goethe, *Faust,* translated by Victor Lange (New York: Random House, Modern Library, 1950), scene 1, p. 25.

2. Edwin Markham, "Outwitted," in *Poems of Edwin Markham* (New York: Harper & Row, 1950), p. 18.

3. Robert Browning, *Saul,* stanza 18.

Chapter Five
Silences You Cannot Safely Ignore

1. Virginia Axline, *Dibs: In Search of Self* (New York: Ballentine Books, 1964), pp. 163-64.

2. Ibid, p. 160.

3. John Bowlby, *Attachment and Loss,* vol. 1 (New York: Basic Books, 1969), p. 28.

4. Paul Adams, M.D., *A Primer of Child Psychotherapy* (Boston: Little, Brown and Company, 1974), p. 90.

5. John Masefield, *Sea Fever,* from *Saltwater Ballads* (New York: Macmillan, 1913).

6. Immanuel Kant, *Critique of Practical Reason,* translated by T. K. Abbott, *Great Books of the Western World,* vol. 42 (Chicago: Encyclopedia Britannica, 1952), p. 360.

7. Antoine de Saint Exupéry, *Wind, Sand and Stars*, translated by Lewis Galantiére (New York: Harcourt, Brace, and World, 1967), p. 14.
8. Francis Thompson, *The Hound of Heaven.*
9. Thompson, Epilogue to *A Judgment in Heaven.*
10. Thompson, *The Hound of Heaven.*

Chapter Six
The Serenity Response to Silence's Call

1. William Ernest Henley, *Invictus.*

FOR FURTHER READING

Coleman, John E. *The Quiet Mind.* New York: Harper and Row, 1971. 238 pages.

You may want an acquaintance with Eastern approaches to silence. John Coleman is a former intelligence officer for the United States stationed in the Far East. He gives an eyewitness report of present practices of Buddhism, Hinduism, Zen and many other types of meditation. He writes in a journalistic style that makes for good reading.

Hammarskjöld, Dag. *Markings.* Translated from Swedish by Leif Sjöberg and W. H. Auden. New York: Alfred A. Knopf, 1964. 222 pages.

What a breathtaking surprise this book will be to you! The harassed, danger-filled life of the Secretary General of the United Nations was sustained at the center by a pensive and prayerful quest for inner silence, peace and certainty. It is an intimate, personal journal kept to be published at his death. Read some of it every day or so.

Hinson, E. Glenn. *A Serious Call to a Contemplative Life Style.* Philadelphia: Westminster Press, 1974. 125 pages.

A practicing contemplative in the workaday world gives an assessment of the problems of devotion in a space age, of appreciating the presence of God in the life process, and of the contemplation of God in the whirl of the day's activities. He devotes a whole section to the understanding of prayer. Most helpful is a whole chapter on the simplification of life. He describes a careful selection of aids to contemplation and a comprehensive bibliography—well selected—for further reading.

Jones, Rufus. *The Faith and Practice of the Quakers.* London: Methuen and Co., Ltd., 1965. 181 pages.

Silence is at the heart of the practice of the Quakers, or the Society of Friends. You may not be "into" any religious group and want to see what people who put silence first are like. This book will tell you.

Kelsey, Morton T. *The Other Side of Silence: A Guide to Christian Meditation.* New York: Paulist Press, 1976. 344 pages.

This author speaks of creating a climate around you for meditation, preparing carefully for the inward journey, using imagery in meditation, and adventuring to the other side of silence. The other side of silence is the meeting with God in Christ.

Kierkegaard, Søren. *Thoughts on Crucial Situations in Human Life.* Translated by David F. Swenson. Minneapolis: Augsburg Publishing House, 1941. 118 pages.

"The man of prayer who loves with his whole heart—it is not without anxiety that he ventures into the conflict of prayer with his God," says this author. He speaks of the quietness after the "conflict of prayer" set off when you face the confession of sin, the occasion of a wedding, and the experience of a funeral.

Kiev, Ari. *A Strategy for Daily Living.* New York: Macmillan, 1973. 118 pages.

A psychiatrist, Ari Kiev, M.D., was asked for a set of guidelines to follow that would help one person living in a small town to face confusion and "keep on the track during times of doubt and indecision." Dr. Kiev set down eight strategies for living and gave a brief interpretation. An excellent way of checking yourself out without paying a psychiatrist for an hour's guidance. A positive and healthy pattern for living and staying well.

Lindbergh, Anne Morrow. *Gift from the Sea.* New York: Pantheon Books, 1955. 128 pages.

A sensitive and meditative expression of a woman to whom the world has not willingly given much privacy. She gives her own story of her efforts to find honest quietude, sham-free silence, and a sense of what is significant to which to pay attention.

Merton, Thomas. *Contemplation in a World of Action.* Garden City, NY: Doubleday & Company, Inc., 1971. 384 pages.

Merton was a Trappist monk who took the vow of silence as a way of life. He found it a way of identifying with the world of action, not escaping from it. This book is one of the longest of his many books. It comprehensively discusses the Catholic mystic's dilemma, satisfactions, and vocation. He says, "Just remaining quietly in the presence of God, listening to God, being attentive to Him, requires a lot of courage and know-how."

——————. *The Silent Life.* New York: Farrar, Straus and Cudahy, 1957, 178 pages.

Merton describes the silent life of the monk in this book. The monk is a person who is called to devote his whole life to seeking God. The person who has been called to find silence in a noisy heart and noisy world while caring for a family, earning a living, etc. will glean from this book a pattern of suggestions for the obedient life of the spirit. He blends the spiritual life into an appreciation of nature, the peace of the early morning, and the quiet of the late night that may prompt you to take a silent weekend at one of the catholic retreat centers, at Yokefellow House, or in your own home.

Nouwen, Henri J. M. *Out of Solitude: Three Meditations on the Christian Life.* Notre Dame, IN: Ave Maria Press, 1974.

In contrast to Merton, Nouwen writes of the life of solitude in relation to caring for other persons on a day-to-day basis. His three meditations are entitled "Out of Solitude," "With Care," and "In Expectation." He helps you seek for "the careful balance between silence and words, withdrawal and involvement, distance and closeness, solitude and community."

Oates, Wayne E. *Anxiety in Christian Experience.* Waco, TX: Word Books, 1971. 156 pages.

Many of the noisy heart's actions are definable forms of anxiety that this book aims to help you identify, get into focus, and dispel. It is a book written at a time in my own life when anxiety was high and had to be dealt with creatively.

_____. *Workaholics, Make Laziness Work for You.* Garden City, NY: Doubleday & Company, Inc., 1978. 132 pages.

If you are feverishly at work all the time, you will have trouble nurturing silence in your heart. You will have a noisier heart. This book aims to assure you of your right to be lazy, how to be lazy in therapeutic and not lethally hazardous ways, and how to get more done with less effort.

O'Connor, Elizabeth. *Our Many Selves.* New York: Harper & Row, 1971. 201 pages.

A practical guide for observing your many selves, both negative and positive, and your management of times when you are critical and being criticized. The practice of empathy as a way of life and the management of your need for empathy in times of voluntary suffering are discussed in ways that enable you to move toward a more serene companionship of your many selves with each other.

Prayers and Devotions from Pope John XXIII. New York: Grossett and Dunlap, Inc., 1967. 315 pages.

The thoughts of one of the most beloved persons of the century are in handbook size here for each of the days of the year. You will "read, mark, and inwardly digest" this book.

Steere, Douglas. *On Listening to Another.* New York: Harper and Brothers, 1955. 72 pages. Reprinted in The Doubleday Devotional Classics, vol. 3, edited by E. Glenn Hinson. Garden City, NY: Doubleday/Galilee Books, 1978.

A profound but simply stated understanding of the power of intentional listening to each other to change the course of life. Douglas Steere is a Quaker. His description of the place of silence in the corporate community of worship is useful not only for a religious group but for any kind of group that takes the need for wisdom as a serious and shared concern.

Thompson, Ken. *Bless This Desk: Prayers from 9 to 5.* New York: Abingdon, 1976. 75 pages.

An executive in a large bank, Ken Thompson has found times of silence and written down what he has felt and learned in the on-the-job practice of private meditation and prayer. Take it to the office with you and read it between times. It fits!

Wessler, Daniel B., and M. Jenelyn Wessler. *The Gifts of Silence.* Atlanta: John Knox Press, 1976. 90 pages.

This husband-and-wife team provides you with a brief set of specific exercises for appropriating the gifts of silence at the beginning, midpoint, and ending of a new day. They speak of silence as a way of life. Silence is a discipline at the specific level of each day's demands. Silence is a breakthrough of the Eternal into the commonplace.